MILLIGAN

HIS PART IN OUR LIVES

Goon bird

SPIKE MILLIGAN

HIS PART IN OUR LIVES

Compiled by Maxine Ventham
Foreword by Shelagh Milligan

ROBSON BOOKS

791·092

First published in Great Britain in 2002 by Robson Books, The Chrysalis Building, Bramley Road, London, W10 6SP

An imprint of **Chrysalis** Books Group plc

Copyright © 2002, 2004 Maxine Ventham

British Library Cataloguing in Publication Data
A catalogue record for this title is available from the British Library

ISBN 1 86105 718 0

Printed by Bell and Bain Ltd., Glasgow

Picture Credits
All cartoons, Spike Milligan
Acknowledgements for use of photographs:
xii, 1, 17, 31, 65, 69, 76, 81, 84, 89, 90, 91, 97, 105, 106, 107, 120, 124, 125, 142, 143, 152, 155, 203 Spike Milligan collection; Front cover, 21, 24, 34, 35, 53, 55, 56, 57 Hulton Archive; 10, 11 (top), 22, 25, 27, 48, 49, 50, 51, 100, 101, 141, 195 Jeremy Robson; 5 Jim Burke, Bexhill Observer; 9 Peggy Edgington; 11(bottom) Keith Smith; 14 Reg Bennett; 41, 45 Max Geldray; 59 Charlotte Robson; 94 David Walpole; 111 Bill Tyler; 115 Barry Cryer; 128 Bill Pertwee; 135 Keith Smith; 139 The *Sun*; 163 Bill Nunn; 167 Tim Motion; 175 Ed Welch; 187 The *Mirror*; 190, 191 Sir John Lambert; 199 PA Photos; 205, 206, 207 Richard Ingrams; 208 BBC.

PUBLISHER'S NOTE

Most of the pieces in this book were written while Spike Milligan was alive. It therefore seemed right to leave these in the present tense.

Not only did this book have Spike's enthusiastic blessing, but he was generous enough to give us a number of his personal photographs for inclusion (some previously unpublished) and to help to choose them. In a few cases he even added Spikeish comments. We are very grateful.

It is a wonderful tribute to Spike that so many of his friends and colleagues so readily agreed to share their stories and memories of this remarkable man. He would have been touched, grateful and amazed – and, we suspect, mightily amused.

Spike Milligan

CONTENTS

ACKNOWLEDGEMENTS

My thanks to Dimitris Verionis for his research, letter-writing and general energy. Thanks also to Sandra Skuse, 'Hern' Dick Baker, Jeremy Robson and Joe McGrath for their help with contacts . I'm grateful to Tim Waters, the Milligan expert, for his knowledge. Thanks to Adrian Briggs for the photo of Bill and his mum. A huge thank you to Shelagh Milligan without whom none of this would have been possible.

Grateful acknowledgement is made to the following for permission to reprint previously published material.
Sir Harry Secombe: *Strawberries and Cheam*, published by Robson Books Ltd 1996, reprinted by kind permission of the Estate of the author.
Roy Hudd: Reprinted by permission of the author and *Yours* Magazine.
Jimmy Grafton: *The Goon Show Companion*, published by Robson Books Ltd 1976, reprinted by permission of the publisher.
Max Geldray: *Goon With The Wind*, published by Robson Books Ltd 1989, reprinted by kind permission of the author.
John Cleese: *Sunday Telegraph* interview, reprinted by permission of the author.
Michael Palin: Reprinted by permission of the author and *Guardian*.
Photographs from Spike Milligan's personal collection, reproduced by permission of Spike Milligan.

FOREWORD
BY SHELAGH MILLIGAN

The first time Spike and I met Maxine Ventham was when we were going to a convention organised by her. She volunteered to come and collect Spike and me and drive us the hour and a half to Brighton. She arrived at the door with a tall American man who was part of the American contingent at the convention. Spike sat beside him as he drove and we had the most hair-raising journey of our lives! This guy had just come off a plane from Los Angeles; he was jet-lagged and in awe of meeting Spike. He forgot which side of the road he was driving on, he went straight through red lights, he went around roundabouts the wrong way and I really don't know how we got there in one piece; it was the most incredible journey!

Maxine hadn't been well and when he found out, this American had literally bullied her into letting him come with her, but I think she was as shaken as we were when we got to Brighton. Even though she wasn't well she decided that she would gently drive us back, much to our relief! We struck up a rapport and as that was not an unmemorable meeting, when she next got in touch with us, we all knew who Maxine was!

After that, she became a dear friend to Spike and me. She stayed with us many times and we shared numerous laughs about that journey. As she'll explain in her introduction, the idea to compile this book came about during one of her stays and it is so exciting for me to be able to look back and remember things I'd totally forgotten Spike had done in the past. There are anecdotes, some of which I was aware of, and those that I wasn't aware of are fascinating and all very believable to me. Spike had such a wide variety of interests and talents that the contributors to this book come from all walks of life; not just famous people, but people who had an important role in his life somewhere along the line. Consequently they all have a story to tell about him.

I hope you enjoy reading them.

Spike and Shelagh celebrate their 10th wedding anniversary S.M. Collection

INTRODUCTION

Since I finished this book, Spike Milligan has died, leaving a huge void in the lives of all its contributors and many millions of others' lives as well. Ironically, I had sent Jeremy Robson the completed manuscript just a couple of days before we heard the sad news. We talked tearfully on the phone and decided that instead of the 'living biography' we had planned, it would make a wonderful tribute to a remarkable man, so we have pressed ahead with the publication.

Spike had given this book his enthusiastic backing and had gone through his photographs with me, which he was lending to accompany the pieces. That was the last time I saw him and, although he looked frail, I never contemplated that I would never see him again this side of the Styx. He loved looking at the photos and making little comments about each one, some of them charming and some witty. Sad, sad, sad to recall now.

You will notice that many of the contributions – those written before Spike died – are still in the present tense; this too was a decision we took, because we believe that Spike is still very much with us through his comedy and the indelible mark he imprinted on his friends' lives. The stories in it are all true and in the tellers' own words. I hope the reader will therefore feel an added sense of satisfaction when reading them, as I did when I compiled them.

Since he had so many admirers and friends, what qualified me to put this book together rather than anyone else? I suppose the short answer is 'nothing'; I was just another friend and admirer of Spike Milligan KBE.

However, I have had experience of his kindness, gentleness, generosity and extraordinary mind at first hand. I first met him properly only five years ago when I organised a convention at which he and Sir Harry Secombe were the special guests. I put 'properly' because I had met him briefly at a BBC function a few months earlier when he had taken my face in his hand and said, 'You're very sweet.' I too had fallen under his spell.

At the time of the convention, I had been suffering with a particularly bad bout of depression and this, combined with my love of comedy, gave us a bond. As for the terrifying journey that Shelagh mentioned in her foreword, Spike swore at the time like the trooper he was, but it seemed to have slotted in with the other bizarre events in his life, leaving Shelagh and me to look back and laugh loudly.

A few months after this meeting, Shelagh telephoned and since then we have kept in regular contact. Later, when she heard I had another bout of severe depression she must have told Spike because early the next morning the telephone rang and it was him. In my surprise I trotted out the standard, 'How are you?' To which he replied, 'How are YOU?' I was honest with him and he asked, 'How would you like to come out to dinner and relax at my house?' Naturally, I told him I'd be delighted and he said, 'Right, see you this evening.' As I was living hundreds of miles away, that was my next surprise. I had expected his call to be a 'sometime in the future' call. How little I knew him in those days!

I duly drove down to Rye. He greeted me in the kitchen with his arms outstretched, gave me a gentle hug and I could have cried.

Later, we went out to dinner and he was the perfect host. I had to sit down while he got my drink. I wasn't to worry about my lack of appetite and was to just relax. When we got back to the house, he wanted to light a fire – so comforting and homely – I must sit down on that sofa and be comfortable, 'There's nothing stressful in this house.' And so it went on. I recall that the weather was glorious and he invited me to swim in the pool, which I did. All very therapeutic.

This sort of care and concern was shown more than once and I grew to see Spike and Shelagh's home as a real sanctuary. Looking back, it was rather like being looked after by a little boy, in some respects. Spike had this charming childlike quality. One morning, he came in unannounced with Weetabix covered with brown sugar and the bowl up to the brim with milk saying, 'I've made this for you.'

At other times his 'Irish, explosive brain' (as he called it) would suddenly come to life and I would be astounded by his profundity or helpless with laughter. His comments while watching television were particularly hilarious. His knowledge of music and musicians was deep, as were his insights into paintings and art.

One evening, not so long ago, Shelagh and I started talking about his effect on people and the help he has given to so many. We pondered the questions: what is it in him that makes him so special and just how important has he been in other people's lives? It occurred to us then that a book, which sought to answer these questions above all others, might give a special insight into Spike. When we mentioned the idea to him, he urged with his usual frankness and enthusiasm, 'Do it!'

When I left for home after my last visit and kissed him goodbye, he said, 'A kiss from a pretty girl, it's not too late for me.' It will never be too late for Spike to win hearts and influence lives.

Whatever it is that puts some people apart from the rest of us – Spike had it. I hope this book will go some way to explain his magic and present everyone who reads it with new insights and stories to illuminate the unique Spike Milligan.

I am reminded of the cry that used to accompany the death of a monarch and it seems very apt now –

SPIKE MILLIGAN IS DEAD – LONG LIVE SPIKE MILLIGAN!

Maxine Ventham
March 2002

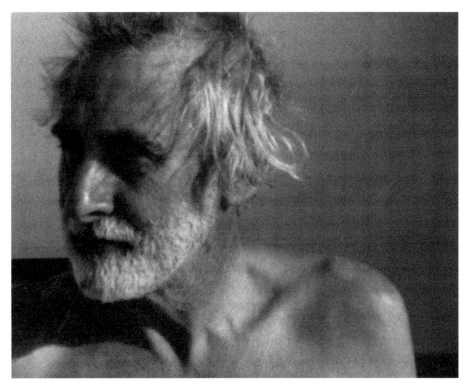

Time off in Tunisia. S.M. Collection

*'*When I look back, the fondest memory I have is not really of the Goons. It is of a girl called Julia with enormous breasts. *'*

DENNIS SLOGETT

Late of D/19 Battery, 56th Heavy Regt. R.A., Dennis Sloggett served with Spike during the war and remained firm friends with him afterwards.

Getting a sight of Gunner Milligan for the first time in early June 1940 was not a particularly memorable experience. He looked little different from the rest of my comrades of D Battery – well, maybe slightly – we all had the rather resigned look of conscripts. Most of us had arrived in Bexhill-on-Sea during March or April so had more or less settled in, whereas Milligan did make a bit of an entrance by arriving alone – and in civvies. Little did we know what an effect he was to have on our lives – even less that we now had a sort of genius in our midst – but this was to become apparent much later, after the war, in fact. But during our service years, first in East Sussex, then in Tunisia as part of the unheralded First Army and so on up the leg of Italy, to us he was just Spike, a comrade who kept up our spirits with his off-beat humour and his musical talents. Of course, the nearer you were to him, the more you felt the full effect, but it spread. In the early days he wasted no time in putting together a jazz quartet of no mean ability. Spike had become our focal point, everybody knew him or knew of him from well beyond the confines of the battery. The band was in great demand for shows and dances and this continued until the time came for the regiment to proceed overseas. But the humour and the music remained a part of our lives.

We were all saddened, no less than Spike, when he had to leave the battery in Italy and it was not until 1960 that further contact was made. This was when Spike sent out a rallying call for a get-together to be held at his office in Kensington High Street. Tracing as many of our old comrades as possible was no easy task. By then most of us had returned to some form of civilian life and Spike had the last series of *The Goon Show* under his belt. We were able to gather together about thirty or so and, appetites whetted, the idea was mooted for a D Battery reunion to be organised. It gradually came together with a small working committee under the ever-enthusiastic eye of Spike.

So, on 7 October 1967, our beloved wartime battery made its reunion debut in a large room above the Printer's Devil in Fetter Lane, EC4. This pilgrimage was repeated annually for the next twenty years. Numbers built up as word got around but inevitably attendances started to fall as time took its toll. We took the decision to move on and to open the doors to our wives and partners – thus we entered a new phase of reunion life at the De La Warr Pavilion in our old second home of Bexhill on 7 April 1973 when Thames TV presented a *This Is Your Life* on Spike.

In the year of the new millennium, we presented our 28th Bexhill reunion with Spike still in attendance, as he had been whenever humanly possible. This year, with most members in their eighties, we made the very difficult decision to call it a day. Previous to this, any mention of making it the last one was met with Spike's opposition, ever the old soldier who could not contemplate any situation justifying such a conclusion. He had been our 'fairy godmother' on numerous occasions, inviting such notables as Prince Charles, Dame Vera Lynn, Anne Shelton and Sir Harry Secombe to be our guests and laying on the music.

Over these last sixty years, he has always been a D Battery boy. How very lucky we have been to have him on our side and as a friend.

'How long was I in the army?
Five foot eleven.'

One of many Bexhill reunions. Dennis Sloggett (far right) watches as Spike and Jack Leaman converse with the Prince of Wales. Shelagh Milligan is on the Prince's left.

PEGGY EDGINGTON

**Peggy was married to one
of Spike's beloved D Battery
soldiers, Harry Edgington.
They both remained great
friends with Spike.**
I was introduced to Spike round about
September 1940 at Victoria Station
when he and my fiancé, Harry, and a
few other gunners from D Battery were
boarding a train to return them to Bexhill, where they were
stationed. It had been their first weekend of leave after several
weeks of training and I was there to see them off.

Through a mutual interest in music and sharing a similar sense of
humour, Spike and Harry gelled straight away and they became
great friends. They spent as much time together as possible, wrote
Goon-like scripts together for their own amusement and formed
a small jazz band. Spike was on trumpet, Harry on piano and they
roped in two others, Doug on drums and Alf on guitar. They were
great. I went down to Bexhill a couple of times to the Saturday
night dances which they ran, Spike being the initiator of course –
and they were a huge success.

After nearly three years of 'defending' the south coast of England,
they were posted to the war in North Africa, after which they saw
action in Italy. Spike was involved in a shell incident in Italy and
was hospitalised, so he and Harry were parted. They didn't get
together again until after the war had finished. They came home
on leave at separate times and Spike came with me to put up the

banns for my wedding. When Spike was demobbed he stayed in Italy, joining two other musicians to form the Bill Hall Trio. Spike was now playing guitar – very well too. And so he entered show business.

Harry went back to finish his apprenticeship as a photo-engraver. He worked at that trade for the rest of his life, while Spike went on to fame and fortune. However, he always kept in touch. Having found success by starting *The Goon Show*, Spike was beginning to make a good living. An early instance of his generosity occurred when we attended a Sunday night recording of *The Goon Show* and afterwards a reception for Spike and his first wife – which went on until quite late. All public transport had finished for the night and we had to get from Mayfair to Highgate. Spike saw our difficulty, without a word being said, and put a bundle of notes in Harry's hand for a taxi fare.

The D Battery band get together: Doug Kidgell (drums), Harry Edgington (piano) and Spike (trumpet).

Spike tried to get some of Harry's original music published. He persuaded the powers that be to include two of Harry's compositions in a *Goon Show* episode. Spike had other tunes of Harry's played on air. When Spike wrote a humorous piece about the starlings in Trafalgar Square, Harry made some contributions to that and Spike made sure that Harry's name was mentioned in the credits. Spike made numerous attempts to help Harry in this way, using his name and connections, the main object being to bring in a bit of money. And so it did. I still get a small amount of royalties to this day.

Over the years, Spike hosted numerous dinners at high-class restaurants, at his home, at Ronnie Scott's Jazz Club. He was, always so generous.

After we came to live in New Zealand, Spike visited us here. On one visit, he gave an evening's performance at a Wellington theatre without payment, to help their ailing finances.

When Harry died, in 1993, Spike had an 'In Memoriam' notice printed in the daily newspaper here, in which he paid him generous tribute.

Spike is a sensitive, kind and benevolent man, and I am proud to know him.

Then came the war. North Africa, promoted in the field (they wouldn't let me indoors). Mentioned in dispatches: nothing positive. Just mentioned.

- Spike on his Army career

Harry Edgington (on piano) and Spike have a musical get-together.

Spike, rehearsing for a Poetry and Jazz Concert, 1962

I used to play the trumpet, I used to try and play like Bunny Berrigan.

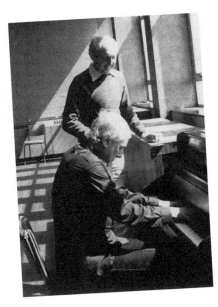

'I compose music, nobody plays it,
but I compose it. '

REG BENNETT

Reg Bennett met Spike during the war, shared his terrible experience with battle fatigue and remained friends with him afterwards.

It was about 1943 and my regiment (74th Medium Reg. R.A.) was resting after the North African campaign.

Despite the fact I couldn't speak French I was ordered to compere (in English) a group of French artists who were to entertain us for two nights. Needless to say, the stage was very much out of bounds for the troops and I was surprised when I approached it for the second evening to find a man playing the piano on it. I asked him what the hell he thought he was doing and he explained that he was the leader of a four-piece band in the 56th Heavy and was wondering if they could play in the interval, to cheer the troops. It was agreed that they could.

Their signature tune was 'Tangerine' and I was completely stunned at the sound they made, particularly the leader who was playing a magnificent trumpet. So much so that I ran like a hare to Kenneth Carter (who had arranged the show due to his past theatrical experience) and dragged him down to the outdoor stage saying that he really must take this band into the show. Needless to say, they were signed up. Who was this magnificent trumpet player? None other than Spike Milligan.

We all went on tour in North Africa and the show was called *Stand Easy*. I used to say to Ken Carter, 'You've got someone there who's going somewhere.' I knew Spike had something special. He was a riot in those early days; you never knew what he was going to do next. His humour was tremendous. That was the beginning of a great friendship that has lasted to this day.

After some time at Monte Cassino, I had been withdrawn from the line suffering with battle fatigue. I was suffering from lack of sleep, I couldn't speak and I was twitching. They somehow put me to sleep for a week and I was sent to a rehabilitation centre where, when I was queuing for lunch, much to my astonishment and pleasure, I heard a trumpet being played and recognised the style. I went over to a tent and there was Spike inside, he had also been sent there with battle fatigue. I broke into tears when I saw him.

He didn't seem as bad as me – he was still very sprightly and full of humour – but he was rather hysterical. He was on the verge of manic-depression; he was, and is, a very, very sensitive man. Originally, he had been sent to a rehabilitation camp at the foot of Vesuvius and he had me in stitches when he told me. While he was there it had erupted and the patients had scattered everywhere! Goodness knows where Spike got to but they found all the men eventually and he had, thank goodness, been sent to the same place as I had.

The treatment consisted of rest, plenty of rest. We went to see a psychiatrist and it was reported that when Spike went there, the psychiatrist went the same way as Spike! We went out every night to vino bars and, with his wonderful sense of humour, he really helped me get over my battle fatigue. Some of the other men were in a terrible state. The boy in the bed next to me was only nineteen. He had been in a tank and sometimes he would sit up in bed and start screaming, poor lad. Spike and I agreed that if we stayed there we'd never get better. I was there no more than six months but when Spike left, I was absolutely devastated.

I wouldn't be at all surprised if Spike's hatred of loud noises stems from his war experiences. A lot of men couldn't stand them. I remember once when there was a firework display, some of the men went berserk.

I did meet Spike again during the war at Taranto, when I went there with a concert party. It was a good war job but Spike maintained that when I was asked if I were better, I should have twitched and said, 'No,' so I could have got a sick pension!

My first meeting with Spike after the war was in 1947. I arrived home one day to be told by my mother that a Spike Milligan had phoned. She described him as 'an excitable young man' and asked me to call back as he had left his number. Unbelievable! I immediately rang him and he told me he was living in Neville Heath's (a murderer) old bedsit and asked me round. When I arrived, he looked like he had stepped out of a Western. He was wearing a red checked shirt, green corduroy trousers and brown boots. In 1947 that sort of attire was unheard of and when we got on the bus to go to a band's farewell concert, I could see the horrified expression of the bus conductor. The band we saw played non-stop till 4am and we sat drinking rough cider. When we left, Spike asked if I had a fag on me and when I replied in the negative, he suddenly bent down and picked up an end off the pavement. He asked me if I had a match, which I had, so he smoked his stub end! We went to a Corner House for breakfast and Spike had the poor waitress so that she didn't know what she was doing.

After that meeting we were both trying to make a living and sadly we lost contact with each other for some years. It wasn't until the 1960s that we came across each other again. I had taken up a position travelling the country and Spike seemed to be in every city I visited with his one-man show. I will never forget the time I met him in Leeds. After the show Spike suggested we join the others at a restaurant called Get Stuffed. Unfortunately, they had left no directions for how to get there. We got into Spike's Mini and I had never been round so many one-way systems the wrong way! How we found the place, I don't know.

My wife and I went on holiday with Spike to Majorca and it was wonderful. We had a marvellous time, something I shall never forget. One evening, we went to a restaurant where there was 'muzak' playing – since the war, Spike has always hated noise – and that was it, we had to leave. He does not suffer fools gladly.

Over the sixty-plus years that I've known Spike, I've watched him grow up with me. Although he's quietened down, he's always been the same character, the same sensitive soul. He's kept his 'ordinary' friends, those out of show business, because he likes the 'real thing'. You can talk about all sorts of things to Spike – music, art, sport – but don't talk about the theatre to him. I believe that even without the war, he'd have had the same talent but his experiences accelerated his talent and indeed his illness. However, I don't think it was his battle fatigue that did that; it was Italy, what he went through there.

It has been a privilege knowing Spike and he still features in my old age; we've stayed great friends but never been on top of each other. Yet we are always there for each other. There's never a dull moment with him. The last time I went to stay with him and Shelagh, not very long ago, when I was leaving he said to me, 'Take care of yourself, you're very special to me.' Well, he's very special to me too.

The RTO gave me a travel warrant, a white feather and a picture of Hitler marked "This is your enemy." I checked every compartment, but he wasn't on the train.
- *Adolf Hitler: My Part in His Downfall (1972)*

Remembrance Day (left).
Spike with war memorabilia (above).

Photos: S.M. Collection

SIR HARRY SECOMBE

Apart from being one of the country's most beloved entertainers – superb singer, champion raspberry blower – the late Sir Harry (Neddy Seagoon) was, of course, one of the legendary Goons. In the second volume of his autobiography, Strawberries and Cheam, *he vividly recalled the heady days of the Goons and more.*

When I first met Spike, he was Lance-Sergeant Milligan, Terrence A, and one of the crew of a large 7.2 gun howitzer, which had been installed in a gun-pit insecurely dug in the hard rock of a Tunisian plateau. His howitzer was being fired by a lanyard – a rope attached to the firing lever which was used when the gun crew was not quite sure of what might happen. As the sergeant pulled the lanyard, the crew turned their back to the gun as it fired, and when they turned round, the gun had disappeared.

At the time I was in an artillery regiment deployed nearby, and I was sitting in a small wireless truck at the foot of a sizeable cliff. Suddenly there was an enormous noise as some monstrous object fell from the sky quite close to us. There was considerable confusion, and in the middle of it all the flap of the truck was pulled open and a young helmeted Milligan asked, 'Anybody seen a gun?'

On a typical *Goon Show* recording day, I would arrive at the Camden Theatre at around 2.30pm, musing on which car Peter had rolled up in. He was always changing his cars. As I entered the stage door I'd sing a burst of 'Return to Sorrento' in reply to which Sellers, lying in a prone position and playing the bongos, would cry, 'It's Singo, the approaching tenor, folks,' and Milligan would announce my arrival with a NAAFI pianist's rendition of 'We'll Keep a Welcome' and a shout of 'Ah! The well-known danger to shipping has arrived. Ned of Wales is here!'

I'd reply with a raspberry and then the jokes would begin – mostly gags of a scatological nature.

Then it was time for our producer to try to exert some control over us (you could tell the producer by the worry lines on his forehead), and get us to have a look at the script. This was the time we all loved best. Peter and I would fall around giggling as we read the script for the first time. Spike would watch anxiously for our reactions to his efforts before joining in the general laughter.

Spike used to drive the studio managers mad with his insistence on getting the sound effects he wanted. In the beginning, when the programme was recorded on disc, it was extremely difficult to achieve the right sound effect. There were, I think, four turntables on the go simultaneously, with different sounds being played on each – chickens clucking, Big Ben striking, donkeys braying, massive explosions, ships' sirens – all happening at once.

It was only when tape came into use that Spike felt really happy with the effects – although I do remember one particular time when he wanted to record the sound of being hit with a sockful of custard. He tried all sorts of ways to get the desired squelch, but to no avail. Eventually, he went into Camden Theatre canteen and asked the very helpful Scottish lady behind the counter to make him an egg custard. 'Certainly, Spike,' she said, knowing that he sometimes ordered fancy meals on account of his weak stomach. 'Come back in twenty minutes.'

When he returned, the canteen lady proudly presented him with an earthenware bowl of egg custard, beautifully prepared with a sprinkling of nutmeg on the top.

'Here you are, Spike,' she said warmly. Spike thanked her and immediately began to take off the grey woollen army socks he often wore. She watched in utter amazement as he proceeded to spoon the contents of the bowl into both socks. She gave a little whimper and ran into the kitchen.

Back in the studio, Spike had already placed a sheet of three-ply near a microphone. Swinging one of his socks around his head, he hurled it against the wood. The result wasn't quite what he wanted, so he did the same with the other sock. Alas, that too failed to produce the elusive SPLAT he was looking for. Realising that he only had two feet and that nobody else would volunteer to try again, he stomped off crying, 'Shit!' because, if truth be known, that was *really* what he wanted the sock to contain.

The only time the three of us appeared on stage together was at the Hippodrome, Coventry. It was the policy of the theatre to put on what they called a Birthday Show in the run-up to Christmas, and we were booked as the headliners.

I was to do my usual performance – a mixture of gags and straight songs; Spike was at the same time still working on his act; and Peter, who was completely without nerves, was experimenting with all kinds of comic ideas because he hated doing the same act night after night. The only piece of material which we did together was a skit on morris dancers (called the East Acton Stick Dancers), which Eric Sykes had written for one of my television shows. For this we wore farmers' smocks and shapeless hats and had bells round our ankles and waists. For some reason best known to himself, Peter appeared as a hunchback, à la Charles Laughton in the film *The Hunchback of Notre Dame*. We also

*We saw ourselves as comic Bolsheviks…
We wanted to destroy all that had
come before and to create something
totally new.*

The Goons, 1951. Left to right, Peter Sellers, Spike, Michael Bentine, Harry Secombe.

BBC Radio 4 presents

THE GOON SHOW

Specially written for the 50th Anniversary of the British Broadcasting Corporation by SPIKE MILLIGAN
Produced by JOHN BROWELL

Dramatis Personae

Hercules Grytpype-Thynne	A plausible public school villain and cad		
Mate	Drains cleared while you wait		PETER SELLERS
Bluebottle	A cardboard cut-out liquorice and string hero		
Major Denis Bloodnok	A military idiot, coward and bar		
Henry Crun	A thin ancient, and inventor		
HARRY SECOMBE	Ned of Wales / Neddy Seagoon / The Houses of Parliament	True blue British idiot and hero always	
Eccles	The original Goon		SPIKE MILLIGAN
Count Moriarty	A French scrag and lackey to Grytpype-Thynne		
Minnie Bannister	Spinster of the Parish and inseparable from Henry		
			RAY ELLINGTON
Ellinga	Batman to Bloodnok, singer and what-have-you		
			MAX GELDRAY
The Conks	Dutch nose swinger and harmonica player extraordinaire		

Orchestra conducted by PETER KNIGHT

Assistant to Producer Martin Fisher. *Production Secretary* Anne Ling. *Sound Team* Eric Young, Maggie Dean, Mardi Eyles, Michael Cowles.
Original members of the Wally Stott Orchestra – Trumpets Alan Franks, Freddy Clayton, Basil Jones, Stan Roderick, Tommy McQuater.
Trombones George Chisholm, Lad Busby, Jack Armstrong, Don Lusher. *Saxes* Bob Burns, Frank Reedy, Harry Smith, E. O. Pogson,
Bill Povey, Ken Dryden. *Harp* Osian Ellis, David Snell. *Percussion* Jock Cummings.
The Ray Ellington Quartet Dick Katz, Judd Proctor, Ian White, Bill Eyden.

Above, part of the souvenir programme for the special Goon Show, *recorded in April 1972 as part of the BBC's 50th Anniversary celebrations – twelve years after the series ended. Among the fans who crowded into the Camden Theatre, London, were Lord Snowdon, Princess Margaret, Princess Anne and Prince Phillip. The Goons' most famous royal fan, Prince Charles, on duty with his ship in the Mediterranean, sent a message: 'Last night my knees fell off with envy when I thought of my father and sister attending the show.'*

carried sticks with bells attached, with which we bashed each other in time to the music of the 'Blue Bell Polka'.

One night Spike had a particularly bad reception from a bewildered audience and, after delivering the immortal line, 'I hope you all get bombed again,' he walked off to his dressing-room and locked the door. He could be heard from the corridor outside as he jumped up and down on his trumpet. After the interval, when the time came for him to join us on-stage for the East Acton Stick Dancers routine, he refused to leave his dressing-room.

Picture the scene as two grotesquely dressed idiots banged on his door, pleading with him to come out, our bells ringing merrily away while Sam Newsome, the theatre owner, the stage manager and the front of house manager wrung their hands in unison.

Meanwhile in the auditorium, the restless citizens of Coventry started a slow handclap.

Eventually, about fifteen minutes after the curtain should have gone up, a dishevelled and unrepentant Milligan responded to our pleading and emerged from his lair. We went on to do our act before a grim-faced audience.

After the performance, Spike was adamant that he was not going to continue with the show, but by the following day he relented and decided to stay on. The only snag was the fact that his trumpet, which was an essential part of his act, was flattened beyond repair and he had to borrow one from the pit orchestra.

Early days: the Goons have problems controlling their scripts.

Right, the title page of a later Goon Show script, signed by Peter Sellers.

Listen, someone's screaming in agony – fortunately I speak it fluently.

Minnie: You can't shoot elephants in England
Crun: Mnk? Why Not?
Minnie: They're out of season
                    - FROM THE GOON SHOW

SERIES 10

PROGRAMME 4

THE GOON SHOW

(Robin's Post)

PETER SELLERS

HARRY SECOMBE

SPIKE MILLIGAN

THE RAY ELLINGTON QUARTET

MAX GELDRAY

WALLY STOTT AND HIS ORCHESTRA

ANNOUNCER: WALLACE GREENSLADE

SCRIPT BY SPIKE MILLIGAN

REHEARSAL:	SUNDAY, 10TH JANUARY 1960: CAMDEN - CAST 3.30 p.m. MAX GELDRAY, ORCHESTRA, RAY ELLINGTON 5.00 p.m.
RECORDING:	SUNDAY, 10TH JANUARY 1960: 8.00 - 9.00 p.m.
R.P.REF.NO:	TLO 5454
TRANSMISSION:	THURSDAY, 14TH JANUARY 1960: 7.30 - 8.00 p.m. HOME
REPEAT:	TUESDAY, 19TH JANUARY 1960: 8.00 - 8.30 p.m. LIGHT TO BE REPEATED BY GOS
F/X DUBBING SESSION:	WEDNESDAY, 6.1.60 AEOL. 2. TLO/CDLO 5385 SUNDAY, 10.1.60 CAMDEN DLO 5454/A
S.M's.	BRIAN WILLEY, IAN COOK and HARRY MORRISS
PRODUCER:	JOHN BROWELL

TEDDY JOHNSON

Singer Teddy Johnson and his wife, Pearl Carr, joined forces to form a successful and highly popular duo and even entered the Eurovision Song Contest, representing Great Britain in 1959 with 'Sing Little Birdie', a record that made it to number twelve in the charts.

In 1951, before *The Goon Show* had started, I was top of the bill at the Brixton Empress for one week. This was before I'd met Pearl Carr and was still solo. I'd had some hit records, although in those days, they were judged as hits by how much sheet music was sold. Those were the last days of Variety. Spike was a long way down the bill and was unknown, certainly I'd never heard of him.

Now, if we'd been in what were called 'the provinces', we'd have socialised but this didn't happen nearly so much at the London theatres. I had been in a local theatre with Peter Sellers and David Lodge and had got to know them well, especially as we shared the same digs, but Spike and I really didn't meet socially then, unfortunately.

He had 'first spot comedy', which meant he followed the opening act, and that was the worst, toughest spot. The audience weren't warmed up at all. I went on last and so didn't get to see him on stage until one night when I arrived early and decided to have a look.

Well, I stood at the back of the theatre and watched his act, although really, nobody could possibly call it an 'act'!! I'd never seen anything like it; Spike was strolling around aimlessly on stage nowhere near the microphone, then he leaned against the side and played the trumpet, still not using the mike! I thought to myself, 'What is he doing on the bill? He's got no act!' The audience reaction was negligible. They clearly thought as I did; this man mystified them. Obviously, he was still trying to find his way in comedy and was far too inventive to be a Variety act. I suppose he felt as Peter Sellers did, who I know hated it.

Only a year before this, in 1950, Dennis Main Wilson had been telling me all about this wonderful team called the Goons, although they were going to be billed as the Crazy People by the BBC. I never associated the man on stage with this team and later, when the Goons were a huge success, I wondered, 'Is this the same guy?!'

He's written such wonderful stuff over the years and now I have his books available to hand, on my shelves, anytime I want them. Anyone who makes you laugh enhances your life and Spike has enhanced mine.

Those 'Crazy People' sign their first contract, 1951. Left to right, BBC Producer Dennis Main Wilson, Jimmy Grafton (in whose pub the Goons would meet), Spike, Larry Stephens (who wrote some early scripts with Spike). Behind them, a cluster of Secombe, Bentine and Sellers.

ROY HUDD

As a connoisseur of music hall and variety, actor and writer Roy Hudd cherishes the night Spike got the boot!

On stage at the Croydon Empire a tall, pencil-thin scarecrow with wild hair, crossed eyes and a peculiar voice was not getting laughs (except from an almost as peculiar-looking teenager – me). My gran, the great lover of comedians, gave a sigh and slumped lower in her seat. The object of the audience's indifference picked up a trumpet and played it pretty well – at least he had a finish. For no reason at all he started to dance while he played – a strange dance – a cross between a storks' mating ritual and a high-kicking tiller girl routine. Suddenly a particular high kick released the dancer's left shoe. It flew into the audience and landed in my lap. It got a laugh. My Gran, ever keen to help, tossed the shoe back onstage. The non-fazed trumpeter picked up the shoe, sniffed it, said, 'Yep, that's mine,' put it back on, finished the number and exited to reasonable applause. That was the first time I saw Spike Milligan.

Years later he rang me ('from the loony bin' – his words) during the middle of a live broadcast on Radio 2 just to say how much he was enjoying the show and that my choice of records was helping him get through a very dodgy period.

For Radio 2, I put together a series of six half-hours called *I Like Spike*. This was my choice of his poetry and prose read by some pals. Again he rang and said, 'I saw the title in the *Radio Times* and thought it was a tribute to Spike Jones and His City Slickers (a famous American comedy band). I love them so I switched on and it was all about me! It's the first time in twenty years I've had a cheque from BBC Radio so you and I are going out for a meal on it.' We did. We went to a restaurant where a great hero of his, Alan Clare, was playing the piano. Spike had brought his trumpet and I sat and basked in the music and company of one of the most special people I've ever met.

Since he shuffled off this mortal thousands of words have been written about the man they called, 'Our only true comic genius', and quite right too. He was indeed a very special wit. Spike's death, for folk of my vintage, meant the death of part of our youth.

Oddly enough I thought of him the day I got the part of Archie the funeral director in *Coronation Street*. In his early days, bored during a day's filming on location, Spike walked into an undertaker's, lay perfectly still on the floor with his arms crossed and shouted, 'Shop!'

When I first saw him, all those years ago, *The Goon Show* had just started to make an impact. To my gran's generation its humour was a mystery. Rather like some of today's comic heroes are to me. It was 'over the top' noisy and anarchistic. Its characters were overdrawn yet subtle, highly imaginative and surreal but totally recognisable. Milligan's words pricked pompous balloons and, best of all, roasted the establishment (you bet that's why Prince Charles was such a devotee). Today's kids think they invented irreverence. Sorry but even Spike wasn't the first. He himself quoted the Marx Brothers, Stephen Leacock, Lewis Carroll and Dan Leno as influences. In turn the Monty Python team, without fail, paid homage to their greatest inspiration – Spike. Today's trendsetters all thank the Pythons. Small world, ain't it?

As usually happens with the death of a popular clown, people fall over themselves to say how loved, and loveable, the said clown was. Spike was all those things but he could be a so-and-so too. I have seen him be extremely prickly, totally unco-operative and behave monstrously. He, like all my favourites, didn't suffer fools gladly. He would go into his shell in the company of mealy-mouthed sycophants and, if people bored him, he could be a rude and uncaring bore himself. With friends, or with folk he admired, he would be just glorious. The sketches he performed on TV would be either brilliant or embarrassing (shades of *Monty Python's Flying Circus*). It was Max Beerbohm who said about another comic favourite, Dan Leno, 'Only mediocrity can be trusted to be always at it's best. Genius must always have lapses proportionate to its triumphs.' It's definitely a small world.

Reprinted from *Yours* magazine

And God said, "Let there be light" and there was light, but the Electricity Board said He would have to wait until Thursday to be connected.

And God said, "Let the earth bring forth grass", and the earth brought forth grass and the Rastafarians smoked it.

A Twit

Is there anything worn under the kilt? No, it's all in perfect working order.

JIMMY GRAFTON

War hero, Grafton's pub owner, Spike's landlord and tutor, comedy brain, officer and gentleman – the late Jimmy Grafton was there at the start of the Goons and helped them all in many ways, as he recalled in The Goon Show Companion.

Spike was probably the most complex member of the quartet of Goons, but as the ultimate mainspring of *The Goon Show*, worthy of the closest study. All the Goons, like most compulsive comedians, were manic-depressives to some degree. Spike's highs and lows were the most extreme, swinging from a state of euphoria in which he was happy, out-going and spontaneously funny, to the complete opposite, when he became brooding and uncommunicative, harbouring dark suspicions and a desire to hide from the world.

Harry decided that I, as an already practising scriptwriter with the added advantage of a pub, was the person Spike should meet. Thus it was that one evening I was introduced to a slim, good-looking young man, whose air of slight melancholy could suddenly erupt into manic glee, often ending in a tearful hysteria of laughter.

His early attempts at written work were an incredible mixture of funny lines and bad spelling, nonsensical padding and nonexistent punctuation; but through it all was discernible the unmistakable promise of great comic talent. Untutored as Spike may have been then, it was evident that the more he learned of his craft, the better he would become. Eccles, I have always maintained, is the real Milligan – his id or alter ego – a simple, happy soul, content for the world to regard him as an idiot, provided that it does not make too many demands upon him.

There has always been a gentle, humanist side to Spike's personality. In those early days at the pub, it took the form of an avuncular attitude towards my children. Spike would often tell them bedtime stories, and to this day they recall the adventures of the Hobbley-Gobbley men, specially created by Spike for their amusement. He also made them fearfully aware of a sinister character called 'Alfie from the Boneyard' who would subject them to unimaginable horrors if they misbehaved. If they were good, they would find little presents from the Hobbley-Gobbley men, hidden about the house. He has, of course, written books for children in later years and has this particular interest in common with Michael Bentine, whose TV programmes and books for children are well known. This gentle and compassionate side of Spike has shown itself in later years by his preoccupation with the preservation of flora and fauna.

Spike's fun was spontaneous. The best example, often quoted, was knocking on an undertaker's door, shouting 'Shop!' then lying down with closed eyes and hands folded across his chest. Vocally, Spike almost always resorted to his favourite character, Eccles. Sometimes this was varied with a strange nasal delivery, which subsequently became the voice of Jim Spriggs, or with a hoarse, rasping voice that must have put a great strain on his tonsils. This was used in later *Goon Shows* for an occasional character called, appropriately, Sergeant Throat.

I have always felt Spike has looked at the world and denounced it as idiotic, preferring instead to create and live in his own world of idiocy. *The Goon Show* was the beginning and perhaps the most enduring part of that world. Many people have enjoyed it, but none more than those (at heart) three small boys who each Sunday, for more than a decade, were let out from the school of life to run amok in the playground of their imagination.

Early days, the Goons performing at The Grafton Arms.

MAX·GELDRAY

The jazz harmonica player Max Geldray featured in The Goon Show *from its* beginnings. Before that he lived and played in Paris with such greats as Duke Ellington and Django Reinhardt. He now lives in America.

The Goon Show did more than revolutionise radio comedy; it revolutionised my life as well. The programmes were all pre-recorded on the Sunday before transmission, and I – with my harmonica – was there, I took part in all the shows.

As part of the Goons I have been asked a thousand times about Peter and Harry and Spike. But I have always been wary of those 'what was he like?' questions, and the very narrow truths they produce. So for a long time, instead of trying to deal with the question, I would answer with a stock set of short anecdotal stories. The stories I told were meant to confirm that the Goons were simply entertainingly oddball characters. They always seemed to satisfy people's curiosity quickly.

Of course the Goon fanatics were a little different. They didn't seem to care for entertaining answers to their questions: what they wanted instead was affirmation of what they believed. And invariably these Goonophiles zeroed in on Milligan.

They would say things like: Don't you think Milligan was the most creative? Or the most eccentric, or the most volatile, or the most crazy. Spike always seemed to be 'the most' something. But the fact is that he is not a convenient entity, and he was always far too complicated and original a personality to be described by a list of adjectives.

I always tend to think of Spike's character visually. I remember seeing him in an English costume drama many years ago, playing the part of a Court Herald. He had on a coarse bulky cloak, together with a hat which resembled an overstuffed pot-holder, and short trunks which were joined at the bottom by an appropriately risqué exposure of fashionable hose. To understate the matter, his was neither an imposing figure, nor a dandy one.

There was a very long and elegant scene in the midst of a crowded imperial court. Our hero stood there shouting something that sounded like heraldic madness. None of the people at court seemed to be listening, so he got louder. Eventually a royal person nodded slightly, and the guard grabbed the herald and carted him off to the dungeons. (As the plot later revealed, this was a mistake; while half of the message had concerned itself with the price of goat meat, the other half was about an enemy army two miles away.)

Why do I associate this scene of Spike the actor, with Spike the man? It's because of the parallels! First, Spike could drive you nuts while he was trying to save your life! Second, those dark and ancient days fitted him as a background much better than anything in the twentieth century does.

Spike seems to me to retain some of the sound and flavour of Poona and Rangoon. I sense it sometimes in the sharp clipped way he speaks. At other times, almost in the way he thinks. Certainly, often, in the way he writes.

I think the time Spike spent serving in the Second World War, and his memory of his father's unhappy experiences with the army (he was unexpectedly discharged when Spike was about eleven, leading to financial hardship for the Milligans, and to Spike – not yet in his teens – having to take on dull manual jobs to help support the family) had a great deal to do with the fact that, throughout all the years of *The Goon Show*, there was a recurring theme that 'took the mickey' out of the military; an officer class he depicted as possessing unlimited degrees of pompous incompetence. One has only to think of Major Dennis Bloodnok, Ind. Arm. Rtd. (Military idiot, coward and bar).

The Goons inevitably met people from all classes, including the highest. But Spike preferred the company of his own pals, whether writers, or just the kind of ordinary people who run his favourite fish and chip shop.

For ten years and well over two hundred programmes, Spike Milligan was the central force of *The Goon Show*. He was the one who forced the BBC into new directions. While there was always a producer on the show, it was Spike who was the manic and inventive driving force behind every detail of the production. I don't wish to take anything away from the brilliant writers who from time to time worked with Spike: Larry Stephens, Jimmy Grafton, Eric Sykes, or any of the others who contributed lines, ideas and whole segments to the programme, but Spike was the special catalyst. And, in this case, that had a very special meaning. Week in and week out, Spike was the central figure in putting all that comedy writing together, 'the tool which fitted and held it all together' as a reviewer once wrote, suggesting that he was the spanner which tightened the nuts and bolts of the other Goons' talent.

Sometime in the early 1950s Michael Bentine described the BBC brass as 'a moribund collection of interfering knighthood aspirants'. That is not to say that they were a group you would characterise as being seriously bad. But they were practitioners of misplaced propriety, and they suffered from terminally dulled sensitivities in every other regard too! Into this unadmirable collection stepped Spike Milligan, appearing with all the panache of a walking unmade bed. A jerk-gaited individualist with a rude tongue. A man whose very smile suggested irreparable calamity. He and they did not mix well.

The impresarios of BBC Broadcast Rules had a no-no list which, though unpublished, seemed to extend over a very broad area. It held that references to the religious, political or military sphere, or to that of the ruling class, were not acceptable in a vehicle such as *The Goon Show*. In addition, the merest satirical mention of the royals was tantamount to treason. This, even though it was widely known that the royal family were great fans of the show. By today's standards, the shows were pretty tame – gentle lampooning, with the odd double entendre and naughtiness thrown in. But that was an age in which some considered even the word 'poop' inappropriate for English ears.

Through the war years, and those following them, this conservatism had cut down on all kinds of creativity at the BBC – and the results were to be heard on the air. There was some fine talent and some very entertaining programmes, but for the most part BBC Radio had a philosophy (philosophy and policy being totally interchangeable words) of 'responsible programming'. It might be argued that comedy programming was prospering, because there was a lot of it and it was suitably decorous and good-naturedly funny.

But Spike was never quite satisfied with that approach to radio broadcasting. He insisted on bringing a wild (if not very imposing) grandeur to mother BBC. But mostly what he brought was innovation!

Later on, this was to become a disturbing dilemma for the upper BBC echelons. They coveted *The Goon Show*'s success, but they hated the unbridled Milligan – and, of course, the necessity of doing his programmes.

I think that, to a man, the Goons and their producers appreciated that Spike bore the brunt of the attack. It was quite a brunt! Arguing over humour! And all that shouting, cajoling, pouting, convincing, brooding, hostility and worry took its toll of Spike. Some of it may still be there, like the unresolved hurt many of us bury inside ourselves. But before your sympathies rise to too high a level, let me tell you that he was a cunning devil too. He would use his reputation as an eccentric to beat down the opposition and confuse them. And I remember that Peter Sellers used to say that Spike had a special gift for explaining simple things so that you could not understand them.

A number of years ago Spike had had his house robbed twice in a very short period of time. Not much was stolen, but he felt that he was a victim, and that the burglars were assaulting the very heart of his personal sanctuary. He walked back and forth in the radio studio almost frothing at the mouth, suggesting he was going to wait for the villains to come back and blow them into little pieces. And he was convinced that they would come back again, for it did seem that there was a pattern to their crimes. Each of the other break-ins had occurred on the last Monday of the month. So, on the next final Monday, Spike armed himself and hid in the shrubbery in front of his house.

Most surprisingly, his instincts proved to be right; there, in the drizzle of the evening air, were two men at the side of his front path.

They came out of the shadows and looked around full of suspicion and caution. And then moved toward a window in his

Strongman act. Spike Milligan, Max Geldray and Peter Sellers in Variety.

dark house. As they got ready to climb up on to the outside windowsill, Spike jumped out of the shrubbery, fired his gun and shouted, 'Got you!'

The villains were so surprised they almost fainted. So the first thing they did was beg to surrender.

When they were brought into court the unthinkable happened. They were let off! As the judge explained, 'Since the accused did not enter the Milligan property, and there is no evidence they intended to gain illegal access, the charge of breaking and entering is dismissed. Since it is not necessarily against the law to look in a window, and we have no witness to or evidence of trespass, all other charges are dismissed. However, while I know that you, Mr Milligan, were armed with only an air rifle – air rifle or no – I am forced to fine you a hundred pounds for the discharge of an offensive weapon.'

I could visualise all this in a Goon script. Spike would turn to the burglars and shout, 'Let that be a lesson to you, varlets! Next time you come to my house you will hang!'

I don't think he should ever be described as a violent man – though for a period in his life he was a champion thrower when frustrated or angry. Even when he was in one of those occasional fits of temper, there was always the sense that there was a line he wouldn't cross – like some pub brawler, who would stop after the emotional release of the first easy punch. I am sure that much of Spike's reputation for temper comes from his face. Spike has always had a profound talent for looking demented.

I remember that once, in the 1950s, a young man at the BBC came rushing up to me, with his face ashen, and whispered that he had heard that Spike had gone over to Peter's apartment with a gun. I am not sure of any details beyond that, or even that this gun business ever really happened. I have no idea what the argument was supposed to be about, either. But I do remember my reaction. I extended my hands in front of me, palms up, rolled my eyes to the heavens and said, 'Oh yeah! So what else is new?'

Couldn't someone have been killed? Or hurt? At the very least, couldn't it have ended their relationship? Not a chance! Hurting each other wasn't part of the game. The next day the two of them were sitting at a table eating crisps and talking about shoes. It seemed that Spike's wife had thrown out all his scuffed-up, comfortable old footwear. He was now about to go on stage and do the show in slippers. Borrowed from Peter.

The most private times Spike and I spent together were in my car. We would be on our way to do a show in a theatre out of town somewhere, and since Spike had not then learned to drive he would hitch a ride with me. Often he would sit there and grumble the whole time. He would talk about the other two Goons as 'Secombe' and 'Sellers', although he always spoke to them direct as 'Harry' and 'Pete'. He would talk about them in a way that was so antagonistic that a stranger might feel that he could hardly wait to get back at the bastards. But that wasn't what it was about.

It was as though he was talking to a brother about another brother. God help someone else if they thought that gave them a licence to start criticising too! It was sometimes a strange loyalty he had to Peter and Harry. Or maybe it was, indeed, a brotherly love.

I cannot recall even one occasion where there was a cruel bite or violence in the thought behind his comedy writing. Instead there was always whimsy, gentleness, innocence and – especially – the absurd.

It was Peter and Spike who developed the characters and fleshed them out on *The Goon Show*. And, especially, it was Peter. Peter was so versatile that if Spike happened to be absent, he could play his own and Spike's characters too. That meant nearly all the voices!

But if Spike wasn't versatile in that way, his gift was that he could always hear and see the characters in his mind. He seemed to know just how the lines would sound on the air. And because of this he always seemed to be able to adapt the lines – perfectly and appropriately – to the character who was saying them.

I remember that I once heard George Burns talking about Gracie Allen: 'Gracie never said funny things, she said things funny.' Spike knew his characters so well that he could make them do both. I think that is why so many of the recurrent expressions of Bluebottle and Min and Seagoon became such well-loved running jokes for the audience.

I would sit there at the edge of the stage and listen to these Goon characters who were like old friends. And then suddenly there would be an old familiar line and almost at the same instant the convulsive laughter would begin. I had heard those lines a hundred times, but I would find myself caught up in the infectiousness – and the laughter would go on and on and on.

When I saw Spike several years ago in London, the only complaint he had about life was to do with work, which he expressed as a complaint that 'those guys don't use me any more'. I'm not sure which guys he meant – he still appears a great deal and is, after all, a bestselling author. He has certainly not been forgotten – and I would measure his success another way. I would measure it by the way his work has endured. Forty years and still going strong.

During the whole of *The Goon Show*'s ten years I never saw any of them drunk on the show. They were too professional, and the show was too important to them, to try and perform half-cut. And if you listen to their incredible timing, their very precise and articulated speech under those heavy comic voices, their control of themselves is self-evident. Besides, Spike Milligan would never have allowed anyone to muck up his brainchild. In fact, very often he would shout at Peter after the show, if Peter had had one of his fits of giggling and hadn't been able to control his performance.

That is not to say they didn't drink at all! If you listen carefully to some of the programmes, when the musical interlude comes and I am introduced, you will hear a voice in the background saying something like, 'Around the back there for the old brandy!' It was a clarion call to imbibe a concoction of alcohol and milk – a combination which Harry Secombe introduced to the group. So, as far as *The Goon Show* is concerned, it can be claimed that I was a cue for the very first 'pause that refreshes' on radio.

Over the years there have been many learned treatises written about *The Goon Show*. There are recurrent suggestions that the Goon comedy is rooted in Lewis Carroll, or the Marx Brothers, or the English Music Hall, or film cartoons like Looney Tunes. But what I saw – over the ten years I was in the show and in the almost forty years I knew those people – makes me think that the comedy was really rooted in the Goons themselves.

Adapted by the author from his autobiography, *Goon With The Wind*.

The Goon Show team, 1953. Left to right: Ray Ellington (whose quartet featured in the show), Harry Secombe, Spike Milligan, Max Geldray and Peter Sellers.

JEREMY ROBSON

As well as being Spike's long-term friend, Jeremy Robson has published several of Spike's books – indeed, he is the publisher of this one!

Sunday night was *Goon Show* night in my family.

I was in my teens when Spike Milligan first came to my parents' home – in fact to see my father, a doctor specialising in hypnosis who helped Spike over many crises, as he was always the first to acknowledge. Over the years our home became his haven and both my parents his trusted friends: my mother's table, coupled with my father's medical and psychiatric skills, were a winning combination!

For me, the enormous benefit was tickets for the Camden Theatre, where on Sunday night *The Goon Show* was recorded before a live audience. Tickets were like gold dust, and the extra one I sometimes had was often a winning card in wrestling a date from a reluctant girlfriend.

At school everybody spoke in Goon voices: Eccles, Moriarty, Bluebottle, Henry Crun and Neddy Seagoon ruled the playground. It's hard to convey the power of radio in those days, and to what extent the Goons permeated our lives. Nobody would miss an episode, or the repeat, and to say you actually knew one of the famous trio was tantamount to saying you had seen the Holy Grail! Spike and the Goons were heroes, and I still have folders of yellowing cuttings from which their indelible faces leap out, timelessly.

Those recordings were wondrously exciting, and the audience warm-up session every bit as enthralling as the show itself. Peter Sellers and Harry Secombe would enter stage right, and Harry would somehow loosen Peter's trousers so that they fell to his ankles, before he launched into a high-pitched version of 'Falling in Love With Love', his fabulous voice spiralling to the Gods. Peter, his trousers now safely up, would move through the ranks of the Wally Stott Orchestra, past Ray Ellington and the jazz harmonica virtuoso Max Geldray, to the drums, whereupon Spike would enter with his trumpet and Dixieland mayhem explode. Then, eventually, on with the show.

Years later, when my wife Carole and I started our own publishing company, *The Book of The Goons* became one of our best-sellers – a volume that featured a genuine correspondence which had been going on for years, in character, between the Goons. Prince Charles came to a private dinner at the Dorchester to launch the book, and sat spellbound as Spike, Michael Bentine and Sellers took off, fencing verbally, topping each other's stories. He couldn't believe his ears! Dear Harry Secombe, whose publishers we were privileged to become, was ill on that occasion but sent a poem entitled 'Ballad of A Sick Ned', which Peter read out. We still treasure a signed menu from that dinner.

But before that, there was poetry and jazz. As an aspiring young poet, full of missionary zeal, I had the idea of organising a poetry reading at the Hampstead Town Hall. For some time, through Spike's introduction to the paper's literary editor, Elizabeth Thomas, I had been reviewing poetry for *Tribune*. As a result I had come to know a number of contemporary poets, including Dannie Abse, who became a dear friend, Adrian Mitchell, Jon Silkin, and Boris Pasternak's sister, Lydia, who had translated her

Wake up Eccles! Top, at the Robson
Books dinner for The Book of The Goons
*Spike greets his Prince, as – in a more
conventional way – do Peter Sellers,
Michael Bentine, Jeremy Robson and
(above) Carole Robson. Left, Spike
petitions HRH for an 'Open University'
Knighthood!*

brother's poetry into English. They were all among the poets I
invited to Hampstead that night. Spike agreed to appear as a
special guest to read some of his humorous verse, and there was
jazz too. I recall that Spike nearly ducked out at the last minute,
but he eventually turned up, amazed to see hundreds of people
queuing down the High Street, fighting to get in. It was a
sensational night, with Spike in rampant form:

> Said Hamlet to Ophelia,
> 'I'll draw a sketch of thee,
> What kind of pencil shall I use?
> 2B or not 2B?'

That Hampstead concert was to lead to hundreds more
evenings of Poetry and Jazz in Concert (as it came to be
called), up and down the country, including a sell-out
concert at the Royal Festival Hall, where Spike again
participated, along with Laurie Lee, Dannie Abse, and
others. I remember that Peter Sellers and Sir Georg Solti were in
the audience: strange bedfellows indeed! Ted Hughes, Vernon
Scannell and Stevie Smith were among the other poets I vividly
recall participating over the years, and often Spike – in his element
with youthful audiences, ad-libbing outrageously, throwing his
papers in the air like confetti, bringing the house down.

All this was to result in Spike getting his own TV series, *Muses
With Milligan*.

So now we go full circle, and with Spike's blessing and his wife
Shelagh's help are publishing this book. Not po-faced however,
not reverentially – he would hate that – but nevertheless with
admiration and great affection. For Spike has touched and in
many ways altered the course of my life (as he has those of
other contributors to this book) and it is good to have the
opportunity to say so.

Having escaped arrest, Spike reads his comic verse at the Hampstead Town Hall in February 1961, the first of many poetry and jazz concerts in which he participated.

DENIS NORDEN

Comedy writer Denis Norden's face is familiar to millions as presenter of It'll Be Alright on the Night. Together with Frank Muir, he wrote a number of radio classics, including Take it from Here and Peter Sellers' great tour de force, Balham – Gateway to the South.

I have an idea that I met Spike through Harry Secombe or Michael Bentine, back in the days when we used to eat in a scruffy little club, because it gave lunch on tick, in other words we didn't have to pay at the time! So, we were contemporaries. I always relished Spike's comedy when I was writing because the more good shows that were on, the healthier it was for everyone involved in radio. *The Goon Show* reached new comedic peaks and the other shows benefited from it.

Spike is my friend and friendship helps people in itself. However, he did help me bring up my children; he had a radio show on Saturday mornings and they loved it. They would sit, listening all the way through and it kept them quiet all through Saturday mornings! I would read them Spike's poems and when they grew up and had children of their own, they read *them* Spike's poems.

I am particularly fond of a line of Spike's which went, 'Anyone can be 52 but it takes a bus to be a 52A!'

There is something about him; as well as his belligerent brass neck he has a fragility that people take to. Anything that is the best of its type appeals to the public – when people stop feeling that, we'll be in trouble. I think he's unique in that he's inspired more bad shows than anyone else. There's only one Spike Milligan but there are innumerable people who try to be but aren't. They get halfway there, are given a show of their own and turn out to be terrible.

When you've known someone for a fistful of decades, it is so hard to describe him or her; it's like trying to describe your right arm. But I suppose if I had to, it would be as admirable and likeable. He is a 'Puckooned reprobate'!

The Goons at the Grafton Arms, 1951 vintage.

MAX BYGRAVES

The ever popular singer and entertainer looks back.

I knew Spike mostly through Harry Secombe, Michael Bentine, my close friend Eric Sykes, and some other comedy writers.

I found him hard to get to know. If I enthused to him about one of his television broadcasts, he'd look furtively around, as if to find an exit quickly, and walk out sideways like one of his Goon characters. Similarly in the fifty years of our acquaintance I never once heard him praise or say he liked another performer. His only acknowledgement to a startling piece of talent would be to draw his cheeks in, suck his lips and lift one eyebrow – as if to say 'not bad'.

Spike never looked for praise, although if a critic rubbished one of his books only by raging, 'I didn't enjoy this book as much as the last one', Spike could dream up swear words about the critic that were so obscene you'd wonder if they were his own invention; in short he could cry blue murder.

But there is no denying he was a one-off, an innovator, a great creator who became a benchmark for future funny men. He also knew his audience and how far he could go.

My favourite story about Spike was when he shared an office in Bayswater with top writers Galton and Simpson, who were

The cast of Eric Sykes' 1954 radio show 'Paradise Street' at the BBC studios. From left to right, the performers are Spike Milligan, David Jacobs, Hattie Jacques, Max Bygraves and the Tanner sisters.

writing the Tony Hancock series. There was also Johnny Speight writing the Alf Garnett hit show *'Til Death Do us Part*, Eric Sykes writing his own top show that featured Hattie Jacques, plus several other comedy authors.

With all this writing output, typists and secretaries were in demand. A new girl had joined the Associated London Scripts team and like the rest of the typists was expected to make tea whenever requested, as the writers would sit around the large table giving each other ideas for scripts and sipping cuppas made from leaf tea.

On one particular day, Spike returned from the loo, went into the typist's room and demanded to know who had put the leaves down the lavatory and not flushed them away.

The whole typing pool stopped typing and eyes went to the new girl. She timidly came to her feet and admitted shyly that she was the culprit. Thinking she was in for a dressing down from Spike, she had owned up. 'It was me Mister Milligan.' Spike stared at her for a moment or two with that steely glint he was known for, then said, 'You're going to meet a tall dark stranger.'

Can't add much to the mass of anecdotage,
only this – at Johnny Speight's funeral
Spike said "I've got Crohn's disease –
and he's got mine"
Warren Mitchell

A scene from 'Till Death Do Us Part featuring Warren Mitchell as Alf Garnett (second from right) and (from left) Eric Sykes, Lorna Wilde, Spike Milligan and Joan Sims.

Announcer Wallace Greenslade keeps a wary eye on the Goons, October 1955.

❛ He said, "Can we have it on a piece of paper, what's the story?" I said, "There's no story." He said, "What does it mean?" I said, "You know, you just get people to laugh. If you've got to make a baby in a cradle laugh, you don't say, "Now here is the plot, you just make it laugh." **❜**

CHARLOTTE ROBSON

**Charlotte's husband Joe was
Spike's doctor, dear friend
and prop over many years.** My husband, Joe, was a doctor who
specialised in hypnotherapy. I often
acted as his secretary when patients phoned home. One day I got
a call from Spike Milligan booking an appointment. I went in to
see Joe, excited, saying that someone rather special was coming to
see him. My husband, predictably, didn't even know who Spike
Milligan was.

It was 1951, in the early days of *The Goon Show*, and Spike was
having trouble sleeping. The pressure of writing a show a week
was an enormous burden for him and his doctor had
recommended hypnotherapy. When Spike walked into the
consulting room he said straight away to Joe: 'I don't trust you, I
have no faith in you but I'll give you a try!'

Well – Joe, being a Yorkshireman, could be equally blunt. 'You
don't have to give me a try,' he said, 'I know what I can do. There's
the door!'

Spike immediately apologised and explained that the reason why
he didn't have faith was because a friend of his had been to a
hypnotherapist who couldn't hypnotise him and had therefore
given him a light anaesthetic. As he was coming round he had
heard the doctor saying, 'and don't forget to pay your bill on the

way out!' This he told to Spike. The same friend repeated this story to me one night at dinner some time later. The friend was Peter Sellers.

My husband had no trouble in hypnotising Spike who would often come over at ten for a session. Sometimes he would stay for a snack of chopped liver and red wine. Sleeping after that was no problem!

Spike with Charlotte and Joe Robson in their garden.

Spike and Joe became great friends and adored one another. Spike was very special to my husband and me. I remember when we went to see Spike in *Oblomov*. The doctor in the play walked on the stage and Spike said, 'What are you doing here, you silly old fool? My own doctor is sitting there in the stalls!' Joe nearly sank through the floor. Spike even dedicated his book *Milliganimals* to us – 'To Dr and Mrs J Robson for helping me during a sticky patch of my life – I used to be a fly!' – we were very touched.

Every Sunday we would go and see *The Goon Show* being recorded. Spike would peep through the curtain to see if Joe was there. The rehearsals for the show were hilarious – better even than the actual shows! I don't think that Spike received as much kudos as the others did at that time. He deserved much more. After all he wrote the shows and was terribly ill as a result of the pressure. I'm glad he got his knighthood.

After the show we would go out to dinner to Le Matelot, near Victoria. Usually it would be Spike and June – Spike's first wife – Graham Stark, Max Geldray, Joe and me and sometimes others. The main object was to try and get Joe drunk. Usually just the sniff of the cork would do the trick! When Joe got drunk the side of his jaw would freeze up and there would be shrieks of laughter coming from our table.

One Mother's Day morning, I was lying in bed, being lazy, when there was a knock at the front door. Someone must have gone to open it because Spike rushed into my room and put some flowers on my chest! I cried out, 'I'm not dead yet!'

We were invited to Spike's second wedding and Harry was there, of course. He said to Joe, 'You think I'm fat don't you? Hit me there!' He was pointing to his stomach. After some protesting, Joe hit him as hard as he could and nearly broke his hand. Harry's stomach was as hard as iron.

We are Jewish and Spike came to a Friday Sabbath dinner, to see what it was like. He enjoyed the lighting of the candles, the wine, the family, in fact he loved the whole occasion. Once he came all the way from the country to our housewarming party and then drove all the way back again. When he came to stay, we liked to get into our pyjamas, open a bottle of Spike's favourite wine (which I still love to drink), a semi-dry white wine from Tuscany – Orvieto Classico Abboccato – drink the bottle and then go to bed. We used to enjoy hearing Spike playing our piano and singing – he had a lovely soft, sweet voice. What was remarkable is that Spike never came here without writing a letter of thanks.

He made our lives much more interesting, of course, and added spice. He also altered the people we mixed with. I was very proud when Spike introduced me to Barbra Streisand; she was at a party we all went to. We also had dinner with Prince Charles, after one of Spike's book launches. During the meal, Spike got up, saying, 'You'll have to excuse me, Your Royal Highness, I'm going to have a pee!' That was a wonderful dinner with so much laughter.

When Joe suffered a stroke, Spike came to see him. He was wonderfully kind and would ring up regularly. After Joe died, my son Jeremy and I kept in touch with Spike and Shelagh, and when we went down to see them recently, Spike kept saying, 'I don't believe it, you're really here!' Shelagh is marvellous with him, a terrific wife and a lovely person.

Spike is kind, extremely sensitive and thoughtful, and is a loving father. He's a really loyal friend if he likes you, but woe betide you if he doesn't! Our friendship has been quid pro quo; I don't think he could have got through those *Goon Show* years without Joe.

SIR GEORGE MARTIN

The acclaimed producer of all the classic Beatles recordings only just got Spike to the church on time.

Spike was never a man for normal small talk, and his wit could have a cutting edge at times. Not long ago, shortly before he died, he rang my home in the country when I was in fact in London. The phone was answered by John Grover, my assistant. When Spike asked to speak to me, John asked – as he normally does – 'Who is speaking, please?'

The reply came sharp as a razor – 'You are!'

I had met Spike through Peter Sellers, with whom I was working in the early 1950s. Peter's main claim to fame was his excellent work as a foil to Ted Ray in the radio programme *Ray's a Laugh*; his film career had yet to take off. I loved *The Goon Show*, and issued an album of it on my label Parlophone, which is how I got to know Spike. We became firm friends, and he used to pour his heart out to me about his unhappy marriage. Mind you, I think it would have had to take a saint to live with such a genius every day. Anyway, Spike and his first wife June eventually separated and in due time Spike fell for another lady, Paddy, who was appearing in the musical *The Sound of Music*. She was singing every night as a nun in the chorus, and I think Spike was dying to get her out of the habit! Eventually he proposed and they decided to marry at her parents' home in Yorkshire. Spike asked me to be his best man, but with the warning that I had to ensure that he did not put a foot wrong. 'Don't worry,' I assured him. 'I will look after everything.' He was especially worried about the impression he would make on his intended's parents, whom he had never met, but had a reputation for being rather starchy and disapproving of show business types.

I knew I had to get Spike up to the wilds of Yorkshire in good time for dinner with them all on a Friday night, the eve of the wedding, so I booked two first-class tickets on the afternoon train to York and reserved a taxi at the other end to take us directly to the house. I had made sure his morning suit was packed with a clean shirt; I even got to check on his cuff links, and I thought I had covered everything. Getting to the station in good time, I went ahead to check the platform number. Only then did I discover to my horror that the train was a Pullman that required reserved seats. I had tickets, but no seat reservation. We were not to be allowed to travel on that train, and the next one would get us in far too late for the family dinner!

I did not know how to face Spike. I went back to the car and was apologetic but brusque. 'Change of plan!' I declared. 'We're driving there.' 'IN THIS?' Spike howled. My only car was a Mini; a boneshaker if ever there was one. 'Let's not waste time,' I yelled. 'Get in, I am going to drive very fast.' So we took off, almost literally, and for nearly four hours Spike clung to the dashboard without a word between us. When we arrived – in good time, I might add – he got out, stretched himself to his full height and with a ghostly white face said to me very calmly, 'Don't ever ask me to get into a car with you again.'

We never did, but our friendship survived. Dear Harry was the only one of Spike's other friends who made the wedding, but it was a lovely affair and it was great to see Spike so happy at last.

We had some great times together. He was a godfather to my son Giles, although he turned up too late to hold him at the christening, so he gave me a tankard for Giles inscribed 'Your nearly godfather'. And nearly a year later, on Giles' first birthday Spike sent him a book inscribed, 'To my Godson Giles, who today is 365 days old, from Spike who today is 18,367 days old.'

Looking back I suppose the records we made were too far out to be a huge success, and in that field he was overshadowed by the albums I made with his mate Peter Sellers. But we did have fun. He was the last and the greatest of the Goons, along with Michael Bentine, Peter Sellers, Harry Secombe – all now Goon but never forgotten – certainly not by me.

'George Martin, of Beatles fame, was my best man. It was a very upmarket wedding, marquee in the garden, all that sort of thing. It was a tiny church, and I remember I didn't like the Moss Bros suit I had to wear, black striped trousers, terribly heavy and old-fashioned. Made me feel like a bandleader!'

Henry Crun

S.M. Collection

MICHAEL WINNER

The highly successful film director has worked with many top stars over the course of his distinguished career, including Marlon Brando, Anthony Hopkins and Charles Bronson. He is also famous for his controversial restaurant column in the Sunday Times.

I first met Spike Milligan in 1953 when I went to see *The Goon Show* recorded at the Palace Cinema, Lower Regent Street. He had been a hero of mine ever since the start of *The Goon Show*. It is difficult to understand today the revolutionary effect this show had on British humour. It was based on the utter lunacy and 'anything goes' attempt to be funny, personified by Spike Milligan. He was and is quite simply a genius. His humour comes from within, from some soul or spirit the like of which we had never seen. The great thing about Milligan's humour is that you feel there is danger in it. Anything can happen. A noise, a repetition of words, non sequiturs, outbursts at variance with reality – all these produce a mesmerising force.

In 1955 when I became editor of *Varsity,* the Cambridge University newspaper, I invited Spike to be one of our guest writers. All my childhood heroes were thus invited, Kenneth Horne who was brilliant on BBC radio's *Much Binding in the Marsh*, Enid Blyton who I'd grown up on – but Spike was definitely my greatest coup. He wrote an extremely witty article and sent us a drawing which I look at now and wonder where the original is! It is a very, very talented cartoon with various people in it and a diagram. I'd forgotten what a good artist he is. The article started, 'Hercules Bleriote snuggled down in his favourite chair, he was a tall man (as you dear reader will observe when he stands up).' In the stuff we printed about the guest writer it says, 'Asked why he was writing this article for *Varsity*, Spike was quite decided: "Because I feel that Cambridge should suffer as I do, when as an Oxford supporter, I watch the Boat Race."'

There is also very great warmth when you meet Spike Milligan. You know you are meeting somebody who has abandoned all the normal inhibitions of social grace and control but is still an absolutely 'with it', decent and endearing person. There is no one anything like him. There is no comedian remotely like him at work in British humour today and I don't think there ever has been. The other Goons had various personae. Peter Sellers could be marvellously lunatic but also very serious and play straight roles. Harry Secombe of course could be a lunatic but also a wonderful singer and a normal musical comedy star. Spike Milligan can only be Spike Milligan. It is a unique performance which he has given throughout his life. Those of us who have been present to witness it for as long as I have are immensely grateful.

I find the big boys who run the film society the squarest things you've ever bloody well met. They've got so puzzled by avante-garde comedy, they label it black comedy. The word "black" is an idiot title; either a film is funny or not funny.

JOHN ANTROBUS

Comedy writer John Antrobus wrote a number of radio shows with Spike over his years, in addition to co-authoring The Bed-Sitting Room with him.

I met Spike in 1954 or 55, I had sent a sample script to Galton and Simpson and they took me on at Associated London Scripts. At the time Spike was also there and Eric Sykes. The offices were over a greengrocer's in Shepherd's Bush Green. When I arrived, a face appeared above, blew a raspberry and disappeared – that was Spike.

We got along well: not only did we share the same sort of sense of humour but we also had a military background in common. My father had been in the army and so had I, just like Spike.

We wrote a couple of *Goon Shows* together. I wish I had done more of them with him but I wanted to be a playwright. I didn't realise they were golden times and how they gave life, I could have been more of a part of it.

When we shared offices, I had a small aquarium and I hadn't really looked after the fish properly. There were only a few and one of them was floating near the surface. Spike saw this and picked up a jam jar, put some water in it and scooped up the fish, putting it in the jar. He took it out on to the street and called a

Spike and John Antrobus at the Mermaid Theatre, during the run of
The Bed-Sitting Room.

S.M. Collection

taxi to take him to London Zoo. I remember that Johnny Speight
and I had a laugh about him doing this.

Spike was gone a couple of hours and he returned without the
fish. When I asked him what had happened to it, he replied, 'The
vet had to put it to sleep.' Well, the image of putting a fish to sleep
was so funny that I burst out laughing and Spike walked into his
office and slammed the door.

One of my favourite stories about Spike – I think he told me it –
happened when he was living at Monkenhurst, his house in
North London. He'd gone to bed early one night when there was

a knock on the door at about 10pm. Spike went down in his pyjamas to answer the door. His neighbour was standing there and said to him,

'I saw you on TV last night – brilliant.'

'Right,' Spike said and shut the door.

About a week later, Spike waited till about midnight when all the lights in the neighbour's house had gone out and knocked on the door. The man came down in his pyjamas and asked,

'Spike! What is it?'

'Saw you mowing the lawn this afternoon – brilliant!'

That reminds me of the time Spike wasn't speaking to his first wife, June. He was upstairs and he sent her a telegram stating, 'Bring me up some soup. Spike.'

When I was suffering from the disease of alcohol, Spike was always kind, there were no recriminations from him, and he was always considerate. When I was in hospital, he wrote me a wonderful letter. Other people being unwell brings out the best in him.

It was only when I was well and strong enough that we had a few difficulties but I believe I am responsible for my own experiences and that I put myself up for it, so I don't condemn Spike. I wasn't very good at standing up to him but that did mean we never had a row in all the years I've known him.

We did a radio series together called *The Milligan Papers* and his contributions could be brilliant. However, he has to be one hundred per cent right, there's no disagreement. If you say, 'No, Spike,' you run the risk of him shutting down the whole enterprise. So, in a way, I was blackmailed because of the consequences of disagreeing with him. If I'd been more robust, I could have dealt better with it. He has the brilliance of a child and the cruelty of a child as well.

We wrote the play, *The Bed-Sitting Room*, together and that was a brilliant partnership. Spike decided we'd direct it but, as he had to play a part in it, I directed it. Shortly before rehearsals, Bernard Miles rang up (it was on at his Mermaid Theatre) and asked if I'd got the set designs prepared yet. Apparently, Spike had said we would do the designs but as he was in Australia and they were needed for Monday morning, I had to do them! I did some drawings and they were OK. That was a tonic for me, to do that.

Spike tried to encourage me to act but I was too shy then, I wish I had done it. He could destroy your confidence on stage if you let him but it was a valuable lesson.

He did a real favour for me by recording my children's story called *Help! I'm a Prisoner in a Toothpaste Factory*, and reading it on *Jackanory*. Spike did it brilliantly.

The reason Spike has remained so popular and beloved by the public is because they don't know him!!!! He had that one coming! We can be friends again now! But seriously, those who do know him do love him.

Spike comes out with some great pearls of wisdom. He once said to a director (not me): 'A cliché is a handrail for the crippled mind.' I remember he also said, 'Children don't grow up, they disappear.' He has a passion that would wake the dead and in England that's needed. Although they still sleep soundly at the BBC!

RICHARD LESTER

Richard, a successful and extremely inventive film and television director, has worked with some incredibly talented people, including Buster Keaton, the Beatles and, of course, Spike.

I did an ad-libbed, live, shambles of a show, which ran between *Dragnet* and a Christmas pantomime and got the fourth highest ratings on television, simply because nobody bothered to turn it off! Peter Sellers rang me about it and we met for lunch and the format we talked about seemed to strike a chord, so we went to meet Spike, this was late December 1955. We found him lying on circular, coiled, two-inch-thick rope on the floor; he never looked up or at me. Peter told him about the planned show and Spike simply said that it wouldn't work and I was dismissed!

However, Peter and I carried on with Eric Sykes and the other writers at Associated London Scripts (Muir and Norden, Galton and Simpson). Eric was also the script editor. The first show went ahead without Spike but I got a call from him after it, 'Do you want to know the running order for the second show?'

The shows that followed were *A Show Called Fred* and they developed a more and more original approach to comedy. They were broadcast live and that's why I went into film directing; where you can do a second take! On one occasion, Peter and

Graham Stark were sitting on a park bench, reading, each dressed from totally different centuries. Under the bench was a St Bernard dog and each man was commenting on the cost of living and trying to work out whether he was dreaming about the other guy and the situation – it turned out that, in fact, they had both been part of the *dog's* dream. The St Bernard had been fine at rehearsals; it wasn't too hot and he was enjoying himself on a day out. However, when the lights were turned on for transmission and the atmosphere heightened, he didn't like it and wanted to go home. Now, a St Bernard who wants to go home is unstoppable: he pulled over the park bench and started whimpering. We were only 22 minutes into the show and I wanted to end but I was told to keep it going. So I told Peter to ad-lib but he was on the floor and helpless with laughter. He and Graham did finally manage to get through the rest of the show with some mumbled ad-libs.

I was totally inspired by Spike's comedy. We all steal constantly from everyone but I would put Spike in my top three or four heroes, with Buster Keaton, Jacques Tati and the man who originally inspired me, Ernie Kovacs. But I have learned more from Spike than anyone else; he taught me to attempt more and to be open to dare more. He forced me out of preconceptions, and encouraged me not to take things at face value – we would go round the back and perceive things from a different perspective. He also taught me what I wanted to do and after the Fred shows I had much better possibilities in my professional life, which was enriched for having met Spike.

I've seen very few moments of genius in my life but I witnessed one with Spike after the first show. He had brought round a silent cartoon and he asked me, 'Does your P.A. take shorthand?' I didn't know, as I'd never talked fast enough for her to need it, so I asked her and she said she did. 'Good, this needs a commentary.' It was a ten-minute cartoon and Spike could only have seen it once, if that. He ad-libbed the commentary for it and it was perfect, I was open-mouthed at the raw comedy creation in front of me.

There were two unexpected events during the shooting of *The Three Musketeers* in Spain in 1973, which happened within a couple of days of each other. Spike was playing Raquel Welsh's husband in the film. I had done this unusual casting deliberately; she made so many demands before filming that it was the equivalent of her throwing a live hand grenade into a room and then entering and asking why no one liked her, which indeed she did ask! So, Spike played her husband and she was dumbstruck when they were introduced! But Spike was absolutely fine with her.

His character was very jealous about hers in the film. We were shooting at La Granja castle. It was night time and everyone was in beautiful costumes for a masked ball, there were coaches and Spike had a tiny scene where he was spying through a very primitive periscope. When I looked at him, I could see he was sobbing. He said, 'It's all so real and they're all dead.' He could see them as the real people of the past who had died and it had moved him to tears.

Two nights later, we were having a drink outside, sitting at a table on the pavement, when a group of Glaswegians headed for us. They recognised Spike and came up, full of affection, and offered him some dope, putting it in the middle of the table. Now, here we were in Franco's Spain, being offered dope – and I had enough to handle with Oliver Reed! Spike declined gracefully and they went away happy. They were a rugged bunch but there was an extraordinary outpouring of affection for Spike when they saw him.

As a man, Spike is courageous and has a generosity that has developed over the years. He's extremely intolerant of incompetence. He is curious in the best sense, like Billy Connolly; they both have a wonderful curiosity to know, to understand and to make sense of life. Spike has taken a great British tradition of treating the surreal with humour and turned it to his advantage but he is a traditionalist, his roots are in Lear and Carroll and the others. I admire him more than almost anyone because of his talent, which is inseparable from him as a person.

He hasn't helped me as a person, I've not been party to his enormous kindness, but I know enough others that have for the case to be proven! If I had felt I needed help I would not have hesitated to go to Spike. Although others may be more outwardly caring, I'd run a mile from them.

I think Spike's best aspect, in my experience, is being funny in a non-calculating, instinctive way. If nothing else, he's made me laugh a great deal in my life when not many people have and I can't ask for more.

Steve Wright (Radio 2 DJ): ❜ You're looking very well, Spike ❜
Spike: ❜ Rubbish, I've been dead for years, and nobody's brave enough to tell me. ❜

❜ I'm just a person –
religion: Roman Catholic,
blood type: rhesus negative,
inner leg: 21 inches ❜

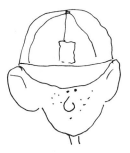

Blue bottle

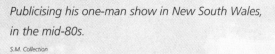

KEITH SMITH

Keith Smith is a veteran actor, whose work with Spike proved popular and productive. Before I worked with Spike, I met him through going to watch the *Goon Shows* with Joan Sims at the Camden Theatre. Later on in the 1950s, I was recording two television shows in the same studios where the *Fred* shows were being filmed. One of my shows, *Click with Keith*, had Peter Sellers on as one of the guests and Spike decided to join us for rehearsals, this would be about 1956. Everyone was very wary of Spike in those days because he had an outrageous reputation and sure enough he was larking about all through the rehearsals, popping up from behind furniture. But, I'm happy to say, he didn't appear in the actual recording.

I used to go and eat at the Trattoo restaurant where Alan Clare was the pianist. He was a mutual friend of mine and Spike's and one night Spike came with his manager, Norma Farnes. He asked me if I'd like to be in his shows – by now he was making *Q* – and I told him I'd love to. Well, weeks went by and I had heard nothing. So, when I bumped into Norma again I mentioned this and asked her about it 'Oh, you know what it's like,' was her reply and eventually, still hearing nothing, I wasn't in his first series.

For the following series, Spike phoned my agent and again invited me to work with him but I was already going to Rhodesia (as it was then called) and didn't want to cancel, so I wasn't in the second series either!

However, Spike rang yet again for the next series and I was in that and every subsequent one. Once, when he called me, I thanked him for the work on Q and he said, 'Don't thank me – you just have a talent for that kind of acting.'

I enjoyed the shows very much, although it was difficult when Spike was down; then it became hard work. He's pretty sensitive to people and I always got a rollicking for talking when it was Dave Lodge who was actually doing it! When Spike was very down and we were just sitting around, he suddenly turned to me and said, 'Keith, play "Laura" will you?' There was a piano in the room and 'Laura' was one of his favourite tunes, a really beautiful melody. I could play quite well in those days and I sat down and played it for him, while he listened. I like to think that helped him.

Spike's intolerance and impatience with people could be difficult to take sometimes and on one occasion I lost my temper with him completely. We were doing a scene where three of us were lined up, ready to be identified by a little old lady. She was an extra, very frail and terribly arthritic, she must have been about eighty. Spike was blacked up as a policeman and said to her, 'Now, walk along the line and tell me which of these men murdered you.' Dave Lodge was dressed as a baddie and had the word 'THUG' written on his forehead. When the old lady got to him, the camera did a close up of his face, the old lady was swapped for a dummy and Dave had to beat up this dummy and then throw it on the floor. After that, the lady had to get into the exact position the dummy had landed in, shooting would begin again and she would get up and carry on along the line to me. We did the take several times and the lady was finding it very hard to get down into position and then get up and carry on, because of her arthritis. Finally Spike asked her, 'Did the director tell you to walk that slowly?' I lost it: 'For God's sake, Spike, she's arthritic and can't go any faster!'

Just then Alan Clare walked on to the set, smiling, and asked, 'Is everything all right?' Spike replied, 'No, Keith's just accused me of being cruel to actors.' We didn't speak at all for the rest of the day, even when we were getting changed next to each other in a confined space. But at the end of the day Spike invited me out to a meal in Mayfair where an Australian violinist was playing (who was awful!) and while we were there he put his arm round me and said, 'Keith, they're all c***s.' It wasn't an apology, it was a 'detour' of one and I never did know to what he was referring. I knew him and I didn't take umbrage but that was a situation that just triggered me off.

It's the same with any genius; the borderline between genius and insanity is razor edge. Spike had his own code of ethics. After one show, I arrived late for a meal and he was having venison sausage. Knowing he is a vegetarian, I was stunned, so he said, 'It's OK, they're culled,' as if that made it all right.
He would ask me if I was drawing the dole when I wasn't working. When I told him I was, he wanted to know if it was enough. I know that he asked Norman Vaughan the same questions and he's a lot richer than me!

He's just a one-off and that's why people love him so much. When I got Spike to sign a book for a man I knew, the guy was absolutely knocked out by it. I phoned to thank Spike and he said, 'It's the least I could do.'

Of course, when he wasn't down he was great to work with and we had a lot of laughs. One morning, when I wasn't feeling at all well, I had to be hung, upside down on a wire, in front of Spike, who was sitting at his news desk. While he tried to read the news, I had to swing back and forth, like a pendulum, and tell him this joke, after which he shot me down. He must have realised I didn't feel well because he offered to do it for me but I went ahead anyway. Afterwards, he considerately came up to me and said, 'Well done.'

He's extremely generous to ad-libs. We had a running gag about a news reader who kept stealing cutlery from the BBC and once, I played a plain-clothed detective and hid a knife and fork on me so that, when I raised my hand, they clattered to the floor. I hadn't told Spike I was doing this and when it happened, he gave a funny look to the camera and then put his hand on my shoulder just as if he were going to arrest me. It was the perfect reaction. 'Keep that in,' he said afterwards.

As a man Spike is extremely sensitive and can be volatile, he's very aware of things and easily hurt. For example, when he was playing Long John Silver, with his leg strapped up, he missed the chair he was supposed to sit on and fell on his backside on the floor. Well, of course, everybody laughed. He got up and ran straight to his dressing-room and stayed in there. Eventually, the director, Alan J W Bell, went in to him and after a quarter of an hour, Spike came out and he was OK again.

I consider him a good friend and a good listener. And, yes, he has changed my life because since he stopped working, so have I!

Spike as Long John Silver.
S.M. Collection

MICHAEL FOOT

The veteran Labour politician and former leader of the Labour Party recalls Spike's involvement with the Campaign for Nuclear Disarmament and a friendship spanning fifty years.

When my wife, Jill, and I lived in Abbey Road we met Spike at the Aldermaston Marches in the late 1950s. We were marching against the madness of nuclear weapons and Spike was there. After the first or second march, we went back to Peter and Mary Noble's house, also in Abbey Road, for a party and, of course, Spike came.

Right from the first time we met him, we were aware that here was a comic genius, who saw the world in a different mode, and we too could see the whole world in a new way through his eyes. Jill had always loved talented comedians, starting with Chaplin, and she knew how special Spike was, so if there was any chance of going out with him, she was in favour of that! These comic geniuses, like the Marx Brothers, Tati, Oscar Wilde and Spike, are all totally original, they perceive things in their own way all the time and unconsciously. In a way, their message in their comedy goes round the world better than drama.

Spike used his genius to fight against the establishment of this country in the 1950s; with *The Goon Show* he changed how people talk about the authorities. Later we went with him to see

Osborne's plays Spike was all in favour of a revolt against the English establishment but, you see, he had been doing it earlier than the others. *The Goon Show* was the proper antidote to what was happening in this country then. Spike found comic answers to questions in order to escape. He came out on the side of the ordinary person, as other geniuses have, but he translated the comic inspiration into modern terms. He was a rebel from the start and he's kept it!

We felt that it wasn't quite fair that people didn't realise that Spike was the inspiration behind *The Goon Show* but he was never jealous of the other Goons. When Peter Sellers and Harry Secombe went on to deservedly make their fortunes, Spike was selfless and glad to see them succeed, even though he had had the genius to CREATE *The Goon Show*.

When we first met him, he would talk about family troubles – Jill and Spike's minds worked in the same way. He was horrified by the way people treated each other and how they treated children. He also suffered terrible troubles with his health, which he overcame heroically. He would ring up and talk to Jill when he felt depressed. She was happy to talk about everything with him and she helped his own efforts to escape his illness.

Spike used to come down to our cottage frequently and was always welcome, no one more so. He became friends with my circle, the CND supporters and anti-apartheid people. My constituency was in Wales and when South Africa came to Cardiff to play rugby, we were all going to demonstrate against apartheid. Spike came down but instead of joining the demonstration he went to see the match! However, my constituents were great fans of his and overlooked this defection!

I don't think I've ever had political quarrels with him. He was very angry when he couldn't get a passport here and I tried to help by

taking it up for him but I didn't succeed and he never blamed me. Not surprisingly, after his disagreements and fights with the English establishment, Spike felt a kinship with Australia, where they treated him well and behaved more sensibly than we did. They understood him better, as indeed they do in Ireland. He didn't have an affinity with the bovine English!

Spike's genius comes out at the most important moments of all. He doesn't allow the rest of us normal mortals to get away with the injuries we commit. There's a serious fierceness in his comedy but he doesn't allow it to take over, he's overflowing with compassion. It's people like Spike who could cure the world of its silliness. He wants to help people and children but not out of conscious do-goodism, he just can't help how he feels, it's in his nature and he was very surprised to discover the world didn't share the same approach as him. But he didn't despair, he came back.

My whole association with him has been nothing but good. I don't know where his goodness comes from – perhaps it's being Irish. He has a different kind of humanity. Some people think of Socialism like that but I don't know if I ever used the ruddy word to him!

Michael Foot congratulates Spike at
the West End opening of his one-man
show.

S.M. Collection

JOE McGRATH

An off-beat film and television director, Joe excels in bringing 'Goonish' creations to the screen. He directed Paul Merton's favourite film, The Magic Christian, which starred Peter Sellers and featured a series of guest stars, including Spike.

I remember reading a critic's review of *Oh! In Colour* (a series that I did with Spike). Contained in it was the line: 'I'm ashamed to admit that I laughed throughout the show.'

Why was he ashamed? Because writers of comedy are thought less of than so-called serious writers? Most great comedy writers, and I class Spike among them, start from the dark side first.

Spike is unique; his speed of thought is terrific, as is his inability to compromise. He told me, 'For years I had listened to those suits in television who told me to hold back, that I was going over the top. So, for a time I concentrated on books and my autobiography, where nobody told me to control myself and one year I outsold Alistair MacLean. From then on, I stopped listening to them.'

Some of the best times I had with Spike were at various restaurants where Alan Clare, Spike's favourite pianist, was playing. Spike's company could, on occasion, be very enjoyable and many of those evenings in restaurants were spent not only with him but also with Peter Sellers, Eric Sykes, Harry Secombe and, through the years, assorted wives and girlfriends. Usually we closed the place and gathered around a piano and as Alan Clare played, we sang. Sometimes, Spike brought along his trumpet, though he claimed he'd lost his embouchure. I offered to help him look for it but he never took me up on that. Once, after asking me to sing one of his favourite songs, he applauded and said, 'Joe, you should have been a musician.' 'Hear, hear,' Pete Sellers called out. I wonder what they meant by that?

Alan Clare was also, in Spike's words, 'the worst actor in the world' and Spike insisted on using him in a television series with a notice around his neck bearing these words. Alan didn't mind this at all. Once, I went to the first night of one of Spike's West End stage shows. Alan came on in a tail suit and seated himself at the piano. Spike entered and did the first half of his one-man show and didn't use Alan. At the end of the first half they bowed and exited together.

The second half of the show followed exactly the pattern of the first half; Alan was never called upon to play by Spike. At the end, Spike called Alan back on to the stage and made him take a couple of 'calls', to the audience's amusement. I went backstage at Spike's invitation. He asked me what I had thought of the show. 'Very funny,' I said, 'Especially having Alan on stage all night and not using him, that was brilliant.' Spike looked stunned. '****!' he exclaimed, 'I forgot *all* about him. I must apologise.' And he rushed off to do that.

You call Spike a genius, Maxine. I looked up the word in a couple of dictionaries and lo and behold, it's derived from 'genie' (as in, 'of the lamp'), an Arabic (Jinee) and Indian (Djinn) word meaning, 'a sprite in Muslim mythology'. As you see, it's from Spike's native subcontinent heath too. And fashionable with it! Genius is defined as 'being a tutelary, or teaching spirit representing the good and evil which attends each person'. Also, 'a being with special mental, intellectual power, possessing instinctive and extraordinary imagination, with a capacity for creation and invention'. Having digested all that I suppose Spike is a genius or the next sprite to it. I must admit, I'd have loved to see him play the genie of the lamp in *Aladdin* (as long as he had written the script). I wonder why he's never done that? I should have suggested it.

The Milligan had suffered from his legs terribly. During the war in Italy. While his mind was full of great heroisms under shell fire, his legs were carrying the idea, at speed, in the opposite direction. The Battery Major had not understood. "Gunner Milligan? You have been acting like a coward."
'No sir, not true. I'm a hero with coward's legs, I'm a hero from the waist up.
Puckoon (1976)

Dennis Bloodnok

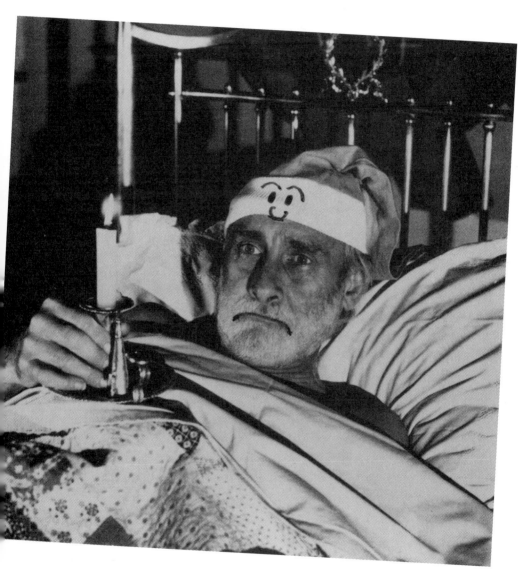

Sleeping on the set (with Spike's inked embellishment).

S.M. Collection

Holiday snaps from Spike's album. In Palm Beach, Australia (above), Los Palmas (right), Tunisia (below), Palma (bottom right).

More photos from Spike's album:
Left, his idea of safety first.
Above, at a Puffin Club outing.
Centre, filming in Vadaland and,
below centre, with Shelagh on a
Black Watch Cruise in 1980, and
(bottom) playing the suitor in
Majorca.

BARRY HUMPHRIES

Barry met Spike in Sydney in 1961 – long before achieving international fame and acclaim as Dame Edna Everage (housewife superstar) and Sir Les Patterson. Spike was a loyal friend to him over the years.

In my very early days as a comic actor in Sydney, so many people told me how funny and brilliant Spike Milligan was that I began to form a somewhat strong resistance to the man and his work. 'You mean you haven't heard *The Goon Show*?' my friends cried in chorus. 'It's right up your street.' Still I resisted.

Funny voices, surreal situations, unbridled sound effects. Mind you, I had adored the Marx Brothers from the start, though such is my nature, I might have enjoyed them less if they had been so heartily recommended to me as were these BBC Goons. At length however, I listened to an episode, and grudgingly, I was instantly converted.

It may be difficult for the present generation to imagine the power of radio in those far-off fifties of the last century. We were Listeners; today's audiences are Watchers. For those who could not enjoy comedy in the live theatre, the wireless was once the only source of performed humour, and in Australia and distant, almost mythical England, it was the radio which provided employment for comics young and old. I had listened to comedy programmes since childhood and was familiar with most of the famous music hall turns who cheered up the empire during and after the war. Now, here was a new kind of radio humour that mocked all the old patriotic conventions and yet somehow, despite its eccentricity, seemed an insouciant extension of the British comic tradition. Not surprisingly perhaps, its principal genius was an Irishman.

When I performed my first one-man show in Sydney in 1961, I was told one evening, just before I went on stage, that Spike Milligan was in the audience. I was understandably nervous, indeed petrified, and when he came backstage afterwards I was surprised to meet such an affable, sane and astonishingly youthful man.

A couple of years later in London, during a brief and poorly received season at Peter Cook's Establishment Club, I was told by a famous astrologer that I would soon be getting good news in a telegram. Within days the telegram arrived. It was from Spike Milligan inviting me to join the cast of *The Bed-Sitting Room*, the stage play by Milligan and John Antrobus which had already opened successfully at The Mermaid and was transferring to the West End. I was offered the leading role of Captain Martin Bules.

Working with Spike was one of the strangest and most exhilarating experiences of my career. If he had been funny on the air, he was even funnier on stage and one could never be sure what would happen from night to night. Spike was given to wild caprices, and one evening left the theatre at intermission without informing the stage management, so the second act began without him, obliging the remaining actors to wildly and maladroitly improvise, until the ill-prepared understudy could stumble on stage and conclude the show before a mystified audience.

Spike during his one-man show in Australia.

Although he was always magnanimous towards me, there was an actor in the cast with a serious gambling problem, who was always borrowing money. Quite often, in the middle of a scene in which this actor was present, Spike would stop the show and warn the audience against lending him money. He was also given, at curtain calls when the artistes took their bows, to pointing out their personal frailties to the audience. Valentine Dyall, whom Spike regularly engaged on radio and in the theatre to impersonate absurdly destitute upper-class Englishmen, was one of Spike's favourite victims, and his private matrimonial torments were communicated to the audience with malicious glee.

Spike was 48 years old at this time and already somewhat grizzled. He had grown a beard for his role in The Bed-Sitting Room but he never allowed it to fully develop so that one might say he was a pioneer of designer stubble. He was also prey to serious bouts of depression and self-doubt. It was also his belief, so he told me, that he had been working as a comedian all his life with scant financial reward, and that his present success in the live theatre had come too late. He seemed unaware of the fact that since The Goon Show, he was already a legendary figure.

His best performance must surely have been Ben Gunn in Bernard Miles' production of *Treasure Island* at The Mermaid Theatre in 1968. William Rushton and I were also in the cast, Willy as Squire Trelawney and I as Long John Silver with one leg and a carnivorous parrot on my shoulder. Spike stole the show every night in a makeup which took at least an hour to apply. His appearance on stage always brought a roar of delight from the kids in the audience and Spike had soon left the text far behind as he went off into a riff of sublime absurdity. In what was meant to be a climactic confrontation, Spike's Ben Gunn drew his pistol and fired it vehemently at the marauding pirates. There was a loud bang and his pistol extruded a limp daisy. When the cheers and laughter from the audience had subsided, Spike cast a conspiratorial glance at the stalls and said, 'See, flower-power.'

Spike maintained a large office in Bayswater which was shared by other comedians and writers like Eric Sykes, Ray Galton and Alan Simpson. He sometimes slept at the office, and at times would visit me at my house in Little Venice where we would talk, drink wine and listen to music. Knowing he was often at my house, his then wife Paddy once telephoned me asking if he was there. Since I knew that Spike had impetuously departed for Australia a couple of days before, I was surprised by his wife's enquiry and I was obliged to tell the poor woman the truth. His mother lived for many years in the euphonious and Goon-sounding district Woy Woy in New South Wales and Spike was a frequent and dutiful visitor; so much so, that he is thought by many people on the sub-continent to be an Australian, a misconception Spike has never discouraged.

He drove a turquoise blue Mini (turquoise was a very sixties colour), and together we often visited derelict houses in London in search of salvageable bric-a-brac. His office boasted a few rather good paintings that he had rescued in this way, though his old Australian colleague from *The Goon Show* days, Bill Kerr, was more enterprising, scouring London with a ladder and a small truck in search of more valuable trove like banisters, large furniture and roofing lead.

At a later point in the sixties Spike, who indulged in many philan-thropic gestures, decided to personally undertake the restoration of the Elfin Oak, an ugly tree stump in Kensington Gardens near his office, upon which some whimsical soul had once carved a host of gnomes, pixies and assorted sub-Arthur Rackham homunculi, and I was briefly his assistant in this thankless enter-prise. Spike's keen instinct for publicity ensured that it received full media coverage.

He had a genius for publicity and rarely dropped out of the correspondence columns of *The Times* and the *Daily Telegraph*. He also, I believe, corresponded with the Duke of Edinburgh of all people, and befriended the expatriate poet Robert Graves who by then was somewhat gaga and may not have fully comprehended the identity of his importunate fan.

Spike generously involved me in most of the things he did including radio shows at which I was notoriously inept. I tended to slow things down by dropping scripts and missing cues and Spike's radio style was fast and furious. This show, including my pathetic performance, may still exist in the archives of the BBC on a long-forgotten Milligan creation called *The Omar Khyyam Show*.

For those unfamiliar with him as a stage and radio comedian, his war memoirs, his novel *Puckoon*, and his children's books attest to his genius. Without him, a whole generation of comedians including the Pythons could not have existed. What a fortunate man I am to have known Spike Milligan.

© Barry Humphries 2002

Carefree in Oz.

S.M. Collection

DANNIE ABSE

The distinguished poet and writer remembers musing with Milligan. I was too old to know about *The Goon Show*, though my young son baffled me with imitations of somebody called Eccles or Bluebottle. I knew it all had something to do with a famous script writer, Spike Milligan.

When a young poet-critic, Jeremy Robson, organised a poetry reading at Hampstead Town Hall he invited me to take part. He told me the poets Jon Silkin and Boris Pasternak's sister would also be on the platform. He did not tell me there would be jazz interludes or that a certain Mr Milligan would perform.

It so happened that because of the unexpected crowds outside the town hall trying to mow down a man shouting, 'Full up! Full up!', I arrived on the platform after the concert had begun. I felt I had come to the wrong place. They were playing jazz. But sitting on a chair stage right I recognised Jon Silkin. Who was the rather impudent, good-looking fellow next to him with lazy hooded eyes?

Suddenly I was startled to see this man step forward and say, 'I thought of beginning by reading a sonnet of Shakespeare's but then I thought why should I? He never reads any of mine.' Who the hell was this, I wondered. Magically naïve verses followed that had the audience stitched.

Jeremy Robson, who became a valued friend, organised a repeat concert at the Royal Festival Hall in June 1961. Three thousand people attended and Spike Milligan (I now knew who he was!) ended the jubilation. I remember how he came rushing on to the stage immediately after I'd finished my stint and the clapping had begun. 'I may as well get all the applause before I start,' Spike said solemnly. Laughter. Then Spike addressed someone in the audience. 'You think, madam, I was joking?' Pause as he peered at the front row. 'Oh – sorry, sir.'

Over the next decade I took part in a number of these Robson concerts and came to know Spike a little. When he fronted a TV series, *Muses with Milligan*, he invited me to take part. In rehearsal, after the actor Hugh Griffith had murdered Dylan Thomas's 'Fern Hill', Spike asked me to read one of his favourite poems of mine, a wedding song. As soon as I concluded the reading, Spike, who'd listened intently, burst out crying.

But perhaps it wasn't the quality of my poem, 'Epithalamion', that had triggered Spike into tears. It might have been rather a reminder of his own difficulty at that time in his life with his wife, Paddy. Temporarily they were not on speaking terms. We learnt that Spike was living upstairs in his house, Paddy down below. When Spike needed a clean shirt he would send her a telegram.

Spike had not only a verbal wit but a very visual comic gift. On one occasion when I happened to visit Jeremy Robson I found him glued to the telephone. 'Spike,' Jeremy said, 'Dannie's just come through the door.' 'Why didn't he open it?' Spike replied.

Coming back with Spike after a TV appearance in Birmingham, I was driving rather fast down the M1. The car window was a little open. 'Is it too windy?' I asked. 'No, but I am,' was the reply. Later we stopped at a motorway restaurant to have a late supper. Before we were even served a woman at another table sent over her paper napkin for his signature. Then another woman did so. Then a man. Then, it seemed to me, the whole bloody lot. The waitress was going back and forth all of a quiver. 'It must be awful to be famous,' I said. 'Yeah,' replied Spike as the waitress vanished, 'when they know who you are you've got to give a huge tip.'

At the Hampstead Town Hall in February 1961; Dannie Abse reads, Spike watches.

Poetry and all that jazz again – at the Royal Court Theatre in London.

GEORGE MELLY

The celebrated jazz singer, writer and expert on Surrealism recalls Spike's surrealist temperament.

Spike and I have known each other now for a long time and, due to his ups and downs, there have been moments when things got very tricky. He, though, is, much more than the other Goons, responsible for a sea change in British humour and from his remarkable powers of invention many programmes such as Monty Python came to exist in a form that otherwise I don't think would have arisen.

I once wrote a review of a programme about Spike's mental difficulties in which I declared him to be a genius. But he is, like many geniuses, and especially those with problems of the mind, entirely self obsessed. He was convinced, for instance, that they had deliberately arranged the collection of rubbish – the banging of bins and the noisy backing of lorries outside his window – in an asylum to drive him even madder. I pointed out this was unlikely.

A few days later, I received a violent letter accusing me of trying to destroy him and asking what I had done for humanity that day (he, apparently, had been talking to an extremely depressed man and had helped to cheer him up) and finally belabouring me for daring to call him a genius. On the other hand, the next time we met when he was on a high and he was amiability itself, much to my delight.

He is a wonderful person, pursued all his life by the furies. It's perhaps conceivable that he couldn't have achieved that truly surrealist invention if he had not been, but one cannot be sure of this. Anyway, I wish him the very best of luck and celebrate the love of his remarkable wife, and raise three loud cheers for the remarkable Spike Milligan.

' Beauty is in the eye of the beholder, get it out with Optrex. '

' All I ask is the chance to prove that money can't make me happy. '

Croonaphant

JOHN FISHER

Producer John Fisher created the popular series,* Heroes of Comedy, *which has featured such luminaries as Tommy Cooper, Ken Dodd and Spike himself.

When the definitive history of twentieth-century British culture is written, no one will loom larger than Spike Milligan. He made us laugh, but did so in a different way. He made us care, but with a sensitivity that so often belied the pain he himself felt.

My first meeting with him, when I was a fledgling researcher working in television in the late 1960s, was nothing if not life-enhancing. More than thirty years and many professional collaborations later, I can state with certainty that he is one of the few truly great men I have ever met.

Eccles

Spike and Shelagh with Princess Alexandra.

S.M. Collection

Left, Spike and Shelagh's wedding on 29 July 1983.

Below, Snapshot from the family album . . .

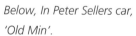

Below, In Peter Sellers car, 'Old Min'.

Above, 'Enforced hilarity' (Spike's comment) – more photos from the Milligan album.

Above, stirring it up at home.

BILL TYLER

Bill Tyler is an architect, a member of the Royal Institute of British Architects and of the Institute of Historic Building Conservation. Having recently left a local authority where he was conservation officer, he is now a consultant specialising in historic buildings.

On the north side of Lodge Lane, a suburban street in Finchley, north London, stand three terraces of highly attractive and desirable cottage-style houses; one of the terraces dates back to about 1820 when the lane formed the northern limit of Finchley Common, infamous for being a haunt of Dick Turpin, the notorious highwayman. In 1970 the cottages presented a very different face to the street. They were run down, some empty and falling into decay and all due to be demolished as 'unfit for habitation' and redeveloped as blocks of council flats.

Spike and his family then lived in Holden Road, part of the salubrious Woodside Park suburb on the west side of the Underground line to High Barnet, and from time to time they would walk along Lodge Lane to the local shopping centre of North Finchley. Spike became increasingly concerned at the state of the cottages, recognising that the appearance of the oldest row marked it out as perhaps being of special historic interest. He contacted the Historic Buildings Division of the Greater London Council, at the time responsible for protecting the most important buildings in London, and was told that 'listing' even the earliest terrace could not be justified. Not one to be beaten by officialdom, Spike approached Jean Scott – the GLC councillor for the Finchley constituency – who was a member of the GLC Historic Buildings Board, which included John Betjeman among its luminaries.

Spike and Jean realised that, without statutory protection of the houses, only by vigorous protest to Barnet Council would there be a chance of defeating the redevelopment scheme. So, early in 1971, a short article appeared in a free newspaper asking for help to set up a local group to carry the fight forward and twenty-five residents subsequently met to form what quickly became the Finchley Society, today one of the most influential amenity groups in the borough. Committee meetings were held in the houses of founding members and it was always a delight to go to the Milligans' large Edwardian house with its long garden sweeping down to the Dollis brook. It was a family home filled with the laughter and the noise of children and sometimes the beautiful sound of his wife Paddy singing an aria or just practising a vocal scale.

My architectural practice specialised in renovation work and Spike generously offered to underwrite plans for a scheme of modernisation to demonstrate to the council that the Lodge Lane properties could be successfully modernised. He came to one of the early meetings with officials who had been vehemently against renovation and, perhaps overcome at meeting such a famous personality, they almost agreed the proposals might have some merit after all. Following very drawn out negotiation and the Finchley Society's inability to obtain charitable funding, Barnet Council agreed that the houses it owned should be transferred to a housing association. A lengthy and complicated building contract meant the first eight renovated properties were eventually handed over at a brief ceremony in 1980, at which Spike, Jean Scott and local MP (now Sir) Sydney Chapman smiled happily for press photographs. Subsequently other owners carried out their own, often rather misguided, renovation work and the whole road clearly shows that you don't have to knock it down simply because it's old, as Spike well knew!

Another of Spike's campaigns involved a remarkable house in East Finchley, again condemned to be demolished but this time for proposed junction 'improvements' to the North Circular Road. 'Hawthorne Dene' utilised forms of construction that may have been the forerunner for similar methods adopted by Sir John Soane for his designs for the great Bank of England complex and Jean Scott became aware of the threat to it through her GLC work. A much more rapid and successful conclusion was reached through its quite prompt designation as a Grade II listed building and consequent substantial amendments to the road scheme.

Early on Spike was made president of the Finchley Society and, following on from Sir John Betjeman, became its present patron. He remained actively involved even after moving from Finchley to 'Monkenhurst', at Hadley Common, when developers finally made life at Holden Road unbearable by demolishing all but four of the grand houses and no doubt offering Spike and his remaining neighbours a price they found irresistible.

At 'Monkenhurst' the committee members of the Finchley Society, and their partners, on one occasion were treated to a splendid black tie supper party as a personal 'thank you' from Spike for all the hard work that had been put in to building up the society to its membership, then of nearly 1000, and for its influence on protecting the environment of Finchley during the 1970s.

His unstinting support for the society was never more evident than in 1973 when he agreed to front a charity show to raise funds jointly for the Finchley Society and, as I have a nephew who is autistic, the National Autistic Society. Spike approached

Spike at the Grimaldi Plaque Ceremony, Finchley Memorial Hospital, 1984.

*'*My father had a profound
influence on me, he was a lunatic.*'*

his friend Sir Bernard Miles for use of the Mermaid Theatre and, under the direction of Michael Bakewell and my wife, Diana, a sell-out audience enjoyed songs from Paddy Milligan, a riotous comedy turn by actor and society member Jonathan Adams (of *Rocky Horror Show* fame) and anecdotes and musical numbers from harmonica virtuoso Larry Adler, accompanied by jazz pianist Alan Clare. Spike arrived at the theatre agonisingly late, with the show well under way and everyone backstage in something of a panic, but still topped the bill with one of his inimitable performances.

Another sell-out fund-raising event at Ronnie Scott's Jazz Club, this time shared with Erin Pizzey's battered women's hostel, was held only through Spike's friendship with Ronnie Scott. His huge range of contacts and friendships have also been called upon to help try to preserve the historic College Farm in Finchley, a late Victorian model farm that is widely visited by north Londoners as a weekend attraction, and for years threatened by closure and redevelopment for housing.

Spike used to regularly attend the AGM of the Finchley Society, chairing the meeting as president; not infrequently there were hilarious moments as he interjected some witty aside, perhaps during the treasurer's report, or as he suddenly departed from the agenda much to the consternation of the honourable secretary. If he could not be there, a note would arrive with his apologies and good wishes, no doubt prompted by his indefatigable manager, Norma Farnes. Norma it was who would field calls to the office, on one visit there providing cups of tea while we – I think it was just Jean Scott and I – waited in vain for Spike to shrug off that day's 'black dog' behind the fast closed door of his room. When such moods overtook Spike at home and he remained closeted in his bedroom, there were few people who could or were allowed to even attempt to communicate with him. One of them was Jean who, at a time when she thought a matter was somewhat pressing, gave me the direct line number for the bedroom 'as Spike wouldn't mind'. I was less than sure about that and, although the number is still in my telephone book, I have never used it.

For years Spike and countless other people have been concerned for the future of Avenue House and its grounds, once the home of 'Inky' Stephens and which he gave to the people of Finchley. Soon it will no longer be managed by the council but run by a new charitable trust drawn from the local community and on which I serve as appointee of the Finchley Society, currently as chairman. So the wheel turns full circle as it were, from thirty years ago when Barnet Council first began to wake up to the fact that perhaps the local community could and would do it better.

Just as the present owners of Lodge Lane owe the existence of their houses to Spike so it is to him I owe the intense involvement I have had with the Finchley Society for over thirty years. As its president I hope to emulate at least some of the example set by both Spike and then Jean as my predecessors. All that has led on to becoming a vice president of the London Forum and being elected as London Regional Trustee of the Civic Trust, the pre-eminent national organisation concerned with making our cities and towns better places in which to live and work – something that I know is held dear by Spike.

I last saw Spike a few years ago when, recovering from his major heart operation, Shelagh brought him from Rye to have lunch before we all attended Jean Scott's funeral service. It was obvious he was not at all well but, being the man he is, he was determined to be there to say his farewell to our dear friend.

To Spike – and to Jean – I am indebted for the interests I have developed and which have enabled me to meet many wonderful and dedicated people. My thanks.

BARRY CRYER

The popular writer and broadcaster recalls some typically Milligan encounters. Having known Spike for some thirty years, on and off – and there were always off moments with Spike – I've collected together a brief nosegay of memories.

He was *Monty Python*, long before *Monty Python*, he was Victor Meldrew, long before Victor Meldrew, but essentially he was always Spike Milligan during Spike Milligan.

I have never known anyone who was so consistently inconsistent. I can hear God saying: 'What's the matter *today*, Spike?'

I was glad to have known him. I doubt if the reverse was the case.

*

A man approached Spike at an *Oldie* magazine lunch and said: 'May I shake the hand of the greatest living Englishman?' Spike replied: 'I'm Irish – fuck off!'

*

I entered the hospitality room of a chat show on Thames Television, before the recording. Spike was sitting in the corner. When he saw me, he leapt to his feet, spread-eagled himself against the wall and shouted: 'Cryer's here! Take my jokes, don't hurt me!'

Spike and I appeared on a radio nostalgia quiz and we were on the same team. On the other team was John Junkin and A.N. Other. The chairman introduced Spike and I and then said: 'And on my right, John Junkin . . .' Spike shouted: 'You mean the coffin was empty?'

With Barry Cryer at an Oldie *magazine lunch.*

The phone rang some years ago. It was Spike. 'Do you want to write with me?' was all he said. I took at least one-and-a-half seconds to accept. He told me that he and Eric Sykes had submitted an idea to the BBC, but Eric was busy with something else and couldn't write it with him. I was elated that, after knowing him for so long, he had even considered me as a partner. But life is badly written. Nothing came of the project. So near and yet so far . . .

*

We did a version of *A Christmas Carol* on the *Kenny Everett Show* and Spike appeared as one of the ghosts. He arrived early on the morning of the recording and I was deputed to look after him. He looked round the studio and noticed that there was an Autocue on every camera. Kenny never learned his lines in advance, but was amazingly quick at picking them up from the Autocue. Kenny entered the show and greeted Spike. 'Everett,' snarled Spike, 'I've been up all night learning my lines and you've got Autocue. Remind me to send you an assassin for Christmas.'

*

One night I went to see Spike in *Son of Oblomov*. He had originally opened in the play, but it had not been too well received. He decided to wreck it and re-title it. The result was a hilarious, ad lib shambles. The night I saw it, after a lengthy pause, he entered and walked across the stage and down some steps into the audience. 'Sorry I'm late, folks,' he said, 'I've had this three-day cancer.' He looked back at them. 'And now for the world's embarrassed silence championships.'

I did the warm-ups for one of Spike's Q series at the BBC. As I stood, chatting to the audience, Spike suddenly walked on, to enormous applause. I backed off, respectfully. He grabbed the microphone and said: 'Van Gogh was Jewish!' and then strode off. Only he would have rejected a punch line – the utterance hung in the air. 'In that case,' I said, 'The rabbi must have had an incredibly bad sense of direction.' It was a knee-jerk reaction. He turned and looked at me. I felt three inches tall. Later, during the recording, he left the building and went to the Tratoo restaurant to hear his friend, Alan Clare, playing the piano. I hope I didn't contribute to his early exit.

*

The day King George VI died, Spike was appearing in variety. He walked on, lay down, with his arms crossed on his chest and announced: 'My impression of King George VI.' History does not record the subsequent reaction to the rest of his act.

> **'I can't see the sense in it really. It makes me a Commander of The British Empire. They might as well make me a Commander of Milton Keynes – at least that exists!'**
>
> *- On receiving an honorary CBE in 1992*

Bloodnok II

DAVID LODGE

One of a vanishing breed of British character actors, Dave has appeared in 115 films and worked with some great, classic stars including Peter Sellers, Sidney Poitier and Richard Widmark. He has also made countless television appearances, some of them with his long-time friend, Spike.

I thought the Goon humour that Spike created was absolutely marvellous and although it really impaired his health at the time, it was so funny. I really enjoyed *The Goon Show* in the fifties. Later on, of course, I worked with Spike on the Q series for the BBC and though I can't say I found it inspirational, being an actor rather than a comedian, I was on the same wavelength. I came to realise the man's madly bizarre, inventive comedy. Anyone who loves good comedy, as I do, must admire his ability to come up week after week with these abstract ideas. Some of the scenes we did were quite amazing. Let's face it: comedy is difficult, drama is easy but at times on Q I was crying with laughter and so was he.

One thing he did for me was to create a running gag, where Spike would come on and say, 'I know you, you were in *Cockleshell Heroes.*' This was the first big film role I did in the fifties and because of Spike saying this in Q in the seventies, it caught on and today people still come up to me and say it. I remember when lovely Peter Sellers died in 1980, and we had a memorial service at St Martin's in the Fields. We came out into the sunshine, walked down the steps and were standing in a little group as a big lorry pulled up in the traffic. This tough-looking guy leaned out and said, 'I know you, you were in *Cockleshell Heroes!*' I'm happy about having that as a sort of catch phrase because it must have made a big impression, comedy-wise and also film-wise.

One of the strange things about working with Spike was that he tried to teach everybody how to perform. I don't think he meant it in a bad way but I'd acted for years and knew my own talents, so I used to listen to him and then go on and do my own thing. I felt a bit angry at first and wanted to say, 'Listen boy, you're not Alfred Hitchcock telling me how to play drama.' But I'd been around him and Peter Sellers for years with their humour and understood it.

I could see he felt the pressure when we were doing *Q*. He would look up at the top BBC producers and swear at them – the language he used was appalling! I have a theory that this is why his shows aren't repeated now; the BBC big boys have a hatred towards him. All of those shows should be shown again, they are so funny and popular all over the world. Maybe they've wiped Spike's shows, I don't know, as he certainly knew how to let rip and his language was always colourful. I remember long before *Q* I was sitting with Spike and he kept using a certain word and I said, 'You have written some of the most lovely poetry, you have complete control of a wonderful vocabulary, why do you have to keep using that word?' He responded with immaculate logic, 'Well, why not?'

This offbeat attitude of Spike's was exemplified by one particular instance I remember. When I wasn't working and my wife, Lyn, was, I used to do the cooking, so that when she came home there was a casserole that could be warmed and ready for her after she'd had a bath. I was preparing this one day when at 4pm the phone rang – it was Spike calling from his office in Bayswater. He asked

Spike, with David Lodge and David Rappaport, in an episode of his groundbreaking Q television series – speech bubble by Milligan. David Lodge was indeed in Cockleshell Heroes! It became a running gag between him and Spike.

me to go and have dinner with him in town and it was obvious he was really down. I had to make a quick decision and I agreed to meet him. When I told Lyn she said, 'You must go if he's down.' She asked me to let her know if I was going to be late and warned me about drinking, because we knew Spike liked to have a few wines. I'd tried to drive home only once like that and I'd bashed the side of my car in trying to get it in the garage, so I wasn't going to do that again.

I drove over to Spike's office and I noticed his Mini when I parked the car. I went in and whereas I was looking very smart in a good suit, Spike was wearing what I can only call a 'John Lennon' hat, a pair of jeans and a strange top. Anyway, we had some tea and chatted for a while before leaving for a restaurant he knew in Kensington. He wanted to take a cab because he didn't know exactly where this restaurant was but we couldn't get a cab and it started to rain. So I announced, 'Forget this, get in my car.' He directed me and when we got there he got out and went straight in, he didn't worry about me!

When I went in, the late, great Alan Clare was at the piano and the management were making a great fuss of Spike. Princess Margaret and Tony Snowdon were in there and Spike, Peter and Harry knew them well. As we walked to our table, HRH looked up and greeted Spike and he said, 'Hello, meet the wife,' which was me! I just nodded and I wasn't even introduced properly.

After we'd eaten, Princess Margaret asked where we were going and Spike told her we were off to Ronnie Scott's and asked her if she wanted to come, which she did. He told her we'd wait upstairs and I thought I'd better ring Lyn to explain what had happened, as it was getting on for 11pm. When I told her, she thought I was drunk at first but then she was pleased for me and wanted to hear all about it when I got home.

When I got off the phone Spike was ready to leave. I asked, 'What about Princess Margaret?' And he responded, '**** it, I'm not going to wait for them.' So off we went. She never did turn up at Ronnie Scott's. Years later, when I was introduced to her, I knew she knew I was the idiot who left without her but she didn't say anything and was charming. That story gives an impression of Spike's mind. It wasn't that he was being unkind, he just didn't even think about it.

One evening Spike and his second wife, Paddy, and Peter Sellers and his last wife came round for dinner with Lyn and me. After a wonderful meal, we were standing in the hall and we were all a bit tipsy, when Spike asked, 'Have you got a piece of paper and a pen?' So, I gave them to him and he said to Pete, 'You are a greedy swine, you had about three rolls, didn't you?' And he went on describing what he ate as we were all laughing, especially as he came up with comments like: 'You kept on using the cruet as well.' Finally he said, 'Well, we've done Dave tonight, I've worked it out at £8.50 each. Good night!' And he left.

The next day, I wasn't working and a black cab arrived to deliver me a letter. It was in Spike's lovely italic writing, he'd put, 'Thanks for a great evening. I've worked it out and it was actually £9.50.' Then the next day another cab arrived and this time he'd put, 'I forgot the VAT!' Now to me that was funny and summed up Spike very well. My only sadness is that I never kept those letters because they were an example of a real turn of wit, which is so typical of Spike, and an expensive gag too!

Two more scenes from Spike's anarchic Q series. Left John Bluthel,
David Lodge and Spike Milligan as unlikely villains. Above, It's a fair cop!
From left to right (seated) Bob Todd, David Lodge and Spike – speech
bubbles by Milligan.

BILL PERTWEE

A veteran and extremely versatile actor, Bill is much loved for his role in Dad's Army.

I met Spike when I was appearing in a television episode of *Beachcomber* or *Q*, I can't quite remember which. I only had a small part, so I was able to watch Spike at work. Actually, I think I did more than one of these shows as I particularly remember one of them for a couple of reasons. I was playing the part of a priest in church giving out communion wine. Spike was one of the congregation and the script had him tasting the communion wine and, after a bit, he would say, 'They've got a better one down at the Methodist; they do a nice (and he quoted a special brand) and other religions . . .' Before the show Spike had been making me laugh, so in consequence I couldn't keep a straight face as I should have done playing the priest. This religious wine tasting went on for quite a while longer as, by this time, I had almost collapsed with laughter and so had the audience.

I had a small part in another sketch in the same show but before we could record it there was some sort of argument between Spike and the director, so Spike left the studio talking to himself and the director then tried to calm the situation, telling the audience there was a technical fault and it would be put right as soon as possible. The audience took it all in good part even though they were pretty sure Spike had disappeared because of a disagreement. The next thing we knew was that Spike had left the studio areas altogether and was sitting in the huge statue that stands in the middle of the whole complex. There is a moat all the way round it. The audience left the building with quite a smile on their faces, I can tell you.

Perhaps knowing Spike has made me realise that you have to have some sort of attitude towards your work, as to what seems right and wrong. But you have to compromise at times, naturally. Perhaps Spike found this difficult once in a while. I realise it is more difficult if you are an inventive, artistic person, which Spike certainly is.

Spike hasn't changed my life but it has been a delight, most of the time, working with him. I say 'most of the time' because the second time I did pantomime with him the production was different from the one we had done the year before in Chichester. To begin with I will explain the Chichester season. It was Spike's first pantomime and he really enjoyed it. The director, Dennis Ramsden, was a lovely chap whom I happened to know and he said to me, 'I don't want to put handcuffs on Spike, I want to give him freedom to enjoy himself and I'm sure we will get the best from him.' He told me to guide Spike through the production and, as I'd worked with him before, we thought this would work. On the first day of rehearsal, the director said, 'Just keep with Bill.' (The pantomime was *Babes in the Wood*; Spike and I were playing the Robbers with Spike playing the Good Robber.) From that moment on the first morning, Spike took my hand and we did everything together. When we got on stage he continued to hold my hand and this seemed to amuse the audience and the other members of the cast. Spike followed the story of the pantomime but he brought his own touch to the regular gags that have been done down through the ages and he also put some wonderful new gags into the proceedings.

Outside the Richmond Theatre, where Spike was appearing in a pantomime with Bill Pertwee.

On the opening night, everything went so well that we were booked to do a similar pantomime at Richmond the following Christmas. This is where things went slightly wrong. It turned out to be a rather different production and Spike was told he must adhere to the new script without adding his own gags. Spike became depressed and this is not very good if you are out there to make people laugh. It wasn't helped by the fact he was put in a small dressing room which only had a window with bars on it (to stop people breaking into the building, of course). It was perhaps lucky that we had worked together before so I could understand his feelings and we just about coped. This situation did not, however, help in his relations with some of the backstage staff, who were upset by some of Spike's behaviour.

When I first saw Spike on stage many years ago in variety he made me laugh on his first entrance. He came on, skipped round the stage a couple of times saying 'Umpi, umpi-dum' as he went and then stopped centre stage and said to the audience, 'I'm getting paid for this and you're paying.' I thought, 'This bloke has a lot of courage.' Especially when you consider that the audience were used to seeing solo performers coming on, going straight into their first joke and continuing with great rapidity for twelve or fifteen minutes.

Spike is now an icon and a little treasure who turned comedy upside down with *The Goon Show*. What perhaps some people forget about him is his talent for writing books. They have all been successful in their different ways and quite rightly so. He's a lovely fellow to spend a couple of hours with and even now can make me laugh.

I think we should remember to thank his wife, Shelagh, for her patient, comforting love in looking after this little national treasure, Spike.

BYRON NILSSON

An American writer whose discovery of Milligan began a love affair with his unique comedy, Byron explains Spike's influence on Americans fortunate enough to have broken into his world.

Spike Milligan was no more than a name rattled off at the end of each *Goon Show* when I first fell under his influence. I knew that he wrote, or co-wrote, each episode, and provided one or more voices, but the first few shows I heard were so difficult to understand that I couldn't begin to appreciate his contributions to them.

Sadly, this reflected the general lack of Milligan appreciation in the U.S.A. in the early 1970s. My journey from curious Yank to ardent fan probably mirrors that of anyone else in the States who discovered and enjoyed the *Goon Shows*. It's a lot of work, or was back in those pre-Internet days, but it also meant you were part of an eager, exclusive club.

As a teenager growing up in suburbia – the New York City suburbs, to be exact – I inherited the community's sense of rootlessness. Few of my friends and none of my neighbours were born in this town; almost none of those who were my age then live there now. Developing a sense of self was difficult. Developing a sense of humour was vital.

Radio, during the late sixties and early seventies, was nearly barren of all but music and news, and a favourite classical music source was a New York City station broadcasting from Riverside Church. Being an affiliate of the Corporation for Public Broadcasting, which funds educational programming, WRVR also aired the *Goon Shows*.

I listened because of an enigmatic listing in a magazine called *FM Guide*. 'The Great Bank of England Robbery,' it began. ''Tis not such a far cry from the respectable Bank of England to a hovel in the Street of a Thousand Dustbins (in London's Chinatown) in whose sinister atmosphere the seeds are planted for the crime of the century . . .' And Peter Sellers was named as a co-star.

The listing made no sense, and the programme itself seemed to make less sense. A rapid-fire exchange of voices, in dialects I couldn't understand, punctuated by rip-roaring laughs at jokes I couldn't fathom. I tried again the following week, and managed to catch a couple of the punch lines. The week after that I tape-recorded the show. As I listened again and again to 'The Case of the Fake Neddy Seagoons', the mists cleared. The dialects grew intelligible. Better still, the jokes emerged, and they were funnier than anything I'd encountered before – because they were rooted in a nonsensical logic that barnstormed through the imagination and demanded that you try to envision the absurd.

Of course Henry Crun was trapped inside a rosewood piano. Where else would he be? It therefore made sense that his every spoken syllable should be accompanied by a muffled note, giving his sentences a plangent melody. Because the context of the episode already was ridiculous, this all made sense.

Sorting out the voices was more challenging. After the musical *Pickwick* was shown on American TV, I knew that Harry Secombe was Neddy Seagoon. Peter Sellers was obviously giving voice to Hercules Grytpype-Thynne, which meant that Spike was the snivelling Moriarty.

Where the Sellers vocal parade gave us a series of well-constructed, even plausible characters, Spike's were just plain off the wall, and thus even more appealing. Bluebottle was the perfect embodiment of the cowardly schoolboy braggart, but Eccles managed to drag a fully functioning alternate universe into his appearances. And poor Henry Crun, piano diversions notwithstanding, had to contend with a housemate who was wont to let rip on the rhythm saxophone, accompanying herself in strangulated rock-and-roll numbers.

Every week I taped *The Goon Show* and went through it several times. I'd never laughed so hard before. I was a goner, and yet I knew practically nothing about the British music hall history that so informs those shows, nothing about England itself and why particular references got such big audience laughs (but to this day I'm nervous about visiting East Acton), nothing about the radio-comedy tradition the Goons so radically sundered. It didn't matter.

I found a list of books by Milligan and ordered them from Foyle's. I also learned that Spike had written a play, which I thought would be fun for my high-school theatre arts class to mount. With teenaged temerity, I wrote to Spike to ask about the play's availability, and managed in an unintentionally snotty aside to ask if those books I'd ordered were any good. A couple of weeks later a letter from Spike himself dropped into my mailbox.

'When you get the seven books,' he replied, far more politely than I deserved, '*You* tell me if they're good, I think they are!!' And he gave publication info for *The Bed-Sitting Room*.

Not surprisingly, the play was far too far-out for a suburban American high school drama group, but Milligan's vision of post-apocalyptic England, with its improbable plot and antic one-liners, was a comforting reminder that a good laugh is more beneficial than any amount of ducking and covering – *The Bed-Sitting Room*, like all of Milligan's work, is refreshingly hypocrisy-free.

It's no coincidence that four of my high school friends and I sought careers in radio work. Although we missed the heyday of American radio, the *Goon Shows* stretched our imaginations and taught us the powerful magic of a pictureless medium. The series ran for many months on WRVR, then ended. Although I'd taped as many as I could, it amounted to a small collection and I knew there were more to be heard.

I was in my last year of high school. An older friend was already working for a radio station situated at a nearby university and known for its alternative ways. If I could secure a contract, he assured me, he'd broadcast the shows.

The timing was good: the school's drama club was about to spend a week in London, attending West End shows. I wrote to the BBC and was told to call at the offices of Transcription House. And so I did. And met, head-on, the organisation that has long been Spike's salvation and bane.

Dressed in a decent suit and tie, hair unfashionably short, accompanied by a similarly attired friend, I thought I cut a convincingly businesslike figure. 'Come in, come in,' said the gentleman to whose office we were conducted. 'Have a seat. Let's have some tea.' In an instant, tea and biscuits were served. 'I'd like you to hear something,' our host said, putting an LP on the turntable in his office.

'We've re-engineered some of the *Goon Shows* for distribution. I think you'll like this.'

What they'd done was force it into phoney stereo, pushing the voices to one channel or the other, racing sound effects across the aural image area. Old recordings, especially in pre-digital days, were noisy. This meant that the noise, too, had to travel; the only way to try to subvert that was to add more noise. It sounded awful.

'That's nice,' I said.

'We think this will make the shows more appealing to the FM market. For how many weeks did you wish to renew?'

Renew? 'We've never broadcast them before,' I replied.

'Aren't you from the Corporation for Public Broadcasting?'

'No, sorry. I'm with a station in Connecticut.'

'What network?'

I began to perspire. 'It's not a network, really. It's just one station. WPKN.'

The BBC man got out his copy of the *Broadcast Yearbook*, a compendium of radio station information. 'WPKN,' he repeated, thumbing through pages. He looked up with concern. 'It's a college station!' he said. I nodded.

He read on. 'It's a Pacifica affiliate,' he said, and this time I heard scorn.

'Well, yes,' I conceded. Pacifica was once a small network of rabidly left-leaning stations that also provided news feeds to sympathetic entities like WPKN. I expected to see the tea service summarily wrenched from the room, but the man recovered and thrust some contract papers and a souvenir carry-bag in my hands and showed us, politely, to the door.

Dispiriting as it was to hear the *Goon Shows* so badly transferred into stereo, some friends and I eventually negotiated a contract that put a brief series of programmes into our hands. And the BBC has gone on to redeem itself with a series of cassette and CD reissues that restore the shows – such as still exist – to their former (and monaural) glory.

Radio genius, underused film star – that would have been acclaim enough, and enough to sustain my admiration. Then Spike's war memoirs began arriving, not to mention the high-spirited *Puckoon*, and I found a new author to collect, with the added challenge of keeping up with a prolific writer whose books never appear over here. And it wasn't only books he wrote: his name turned up as the author of liner notes to jazz recordings – and his war memoirs filled out the background of Milligan the trumpet player.

When I learned he was a fan of Bunny Berrigan and other classic musicians, I sent him some tapes of reissues I'd recently collected. In his replies, he mentioned his sadness at

> . . . the gradual decreasing, on a world-wide scale, of music of this ilk as used by the pop-orientated raging radio stations. On television, of course, jazz is dead dead dead. I cannot understand the mentality, but I loathe it whatever it is.

In another letter he noted that

> . . . 'modern' popular music is the pits to me, it's as welcome as Hitler in a synagogue. Ninety-nine per cent of people know or feel bugger-all. Recently I started composing music, at a dinner party one of the guests requested I play a tape of it. I put it on, they talked all the way through and then said 'Lovely'. Bullshit! I played some to [jazz trumpeter] Warren Vaché – and he listened, better still he liked it, and took a few tunes with the intention of playing them, so I was well pleased.

Eventually I also became aware of Milligan the environmentalist. Hollywood stars as political activists has become something of a cliché, carrying a side-image of wealthy actors with too much free time trying to assuage their guilt over being so rich from doing so little. Milligan's example was a far different story. Here was a man clearly and passionately committed to the cause, who lived the precepts he preached. I have read and heard his opinions not only on the terrible abuse of nature and natural resources, but also complaints that range from noise pollution to overpopulation. He couldn't be more correct, and his was one of the voices that persuaded my wife and me to enhance our family with but one child.

When I hear my five-year-old daughter sing 'On the Ning Nang Nong', I feel a terrific pleasure at having passed along Spike's legacy. As a writer of children's stories and poems – and a performer of same – he's unsurpassed.

So much of what passes for children's literature is just the work of a hack not good enough to pen decent fiction, condescending to a misguided idea of how children speak among themselves – and therefore just as ineffective (and damaging) as baby talk. Milligan's work speaks directly to kids, treating them as equals while playing to their wonderfully uncensored sense of the absurd. Rather than presenting a preconceived world view, Spike's work teaches them dangerous things like thinking for themselves and laughing at the bureaucratic forces that want to imprison their impulses. I envy those in his native country who have grown up with easy access to his influence.

Thanks to the popularity of *Monty Python's Flying Circus* on American television, British comedy has been more accessible in terms both of acquisition and understanding. I think a sixteen-year-old American today has an easier time figuring out the *Goon Shows* than I had all those years ago. And I've tried to do my share to pass along the legacy, which means that there's a sizeable quantity of books and tapes in circulation that I doubt I'll ever see returned.

'Do they still play the Goon Shows in America?' Spike asked in one of his letters. 'I can't believe it! I mean, it's 34 years since they started.' I don't doubt that he's sincerely surprised, but he's also far too modest. More than one English friend has characterised Milligan as a national treasure, and you're lucky to have him in your midst. Over here it's been a challenge to keep up, but, as with all challenges, the effort of remaining a fan has been all the sweeter for costing that effort.

JOANNA LUMLEY

One of Britain's most versatile and popular actresses, Joanna is now particularly loved for her portrayal of Patsy in Absolutely Fabulous.

I first saw Spike's personal magic in action at the end of an anti-whaling rally in Trafalgar Square in the seventies. As the huge crowd dispersed, some autograph hunters approached Spike, holding pens and scraps of paper. Leaning on the base of one of Landseer's great lions, he wrote beautifully and carefully in his distinctive italic handwriting, with a short message ('with best wishes' or something like it), inscribing their name and his own signature with infinite patience. This took some time; he was surrounded by eager fans but he didn't scribble or go faster – each autograph hunter went away with a real treasure and a feeling that Spike, for a moment, had concentrated only on them. Other stars were rushed into waiting cars, the square emptied but Spike wrote on. When he had finished, he walked off alone.

He is completely without artifice, completely untouched by fame, glamour and riches. He is hysterically funny, gentle, furious, philosophical, unpredictable and (of course) a genius. He is as kind as kind can be, and he is my friend and my hero.

The Sun pays imaginative tribute to Spike's genius. Reproduced by kind permission of the editor, David Yelland, who wrote: 'I would be more than honoured for this to happen. In fact, I'm delighted to get such a message. I loved Spike.'

MICHAEL PARKINSON

The stalwart talk show host, generally recognised as the master of the art, interviewed Spike on a number of occasions – never easy!

My favourite anecdote about Spike has to do with a magazine article in which my mother was referred to as 'an old cow'. This was some time in the seventies and, as you can imagine, it greatly upset me. I thought about writing and complaining and then thought again. I would only give them the kind of publicity they craved and enable them to repeat the insult. Anyway, a couple of weeks later in the 'letters' column of the same magazine was a letter to the editor from Spike, which said:

Dear Sir, I am the mother of Michael Parkinson and I dislike being called an old cow . . .

It was a funny, mad, wonderful letter which made a complete nonsense of what they had written and, moreover, deflected the insult to my mother. It enabled me to write the next week complaining that Spike was not my mother and you can imagine what transpired after that. He didn't have to do it but did because instinctively he is a kind man and a great friend.

He was the presiding genius behind the Goons. But he was an awkward man in many ways, and was not easy to get on with.

If he took against you, watch out! I got on with him very well. People assumed he was God's gift to talk shows, but he wasn't. He could veer from being absolutely obnoxious to being wonderful, depending on the mood you found him in.

Once when I was live on a radio show, I received a call from someone who said: 'Spike is here to see you.' He just came into the studio, in his dressing gown, was brilliant for an hour, and then went back to his clinic. An extraordinary man.

Michael Parkinson at the launch party for The Book of The Goons. *Spike signs copies.*

*Spike and his mum
(above).*

*All dressed up for
Charles and Di's
royal wedding
(right).*

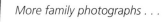

More family photographs . . .

Photos: S.M. Collection

MARIA ANTONIETTA PONTANI

**By Spike's own admission,
Maria was a great early love.**

In fact, it's a long time I have loved and appreciated Terry Milligan . . . since 1945! But I don't think there is any 'witchcraft' about his success. Terry is just a great artist. He plays many instruments, interprets various characters, invents plays written with such a particular sense of humour and his drawings show a fabulous imagination!

And still, although he has so many talents, he remains a deeply human person, kind and aware of true values. Success hasn't changed his soul or his heart. That is why I deeply love Terry Milligan!

FABIANA CIFUENTES (HER DAUGHTER)

In 1973, I came to England for my studies. My boyfriend at that time, Peter, was a great fan of Spike Milligan and Bob Dylan. He played the guitar beautifully. He was a funny character himself and used to call me 'Harold'! One Christmas, he gave me plenty of books by Spike in order to cheer me up from the cold I was going to endure in Belgrade, where my parents lived at that period.

As soon as I arrived, I showed them enthusiastically to my parents . . . and that's how my mother and Terry met after 30 years of silence!

Drinking partners – Michael Bentine (above) and Peter Sellers (below).

❜[Peter Sellers and I] were very close together.
I knew whatever I wrote he would appreciate it
to the maximum. He would say so. "A very funny script,
Spike, a very funny script." It was very
good for the ego. That did help to ease the
mental pain. ❜

GARY MORECAMBE

Writer, novelist and biographer, Gary recently completed a book on his father, another comedy great, Eric Morecambe.

Spike was one of my father Eric Morecambe's few contemporary heroes. Eric admired much of his work. He also felt that Spike suffered for his talent, and that it therefore followed he could be regarded as a genuine comic genius, something Eric dismissed when he himself was often described in a similar way. Indeed, Eric once told me that Spike was the only comic genius he could think of, though he did confess to having immense regard for Spike's fellow-Goon, Peter Sellers.

Following a Morecambe and Wise Christmas special in the mid-seventies, when Des O'Connor was a guest star on the show, Spike wrote to Eric. He congratulated him on the show, but added they had missed a great line. When Des said he'd like to sing on their show, Spike reckoned that Eric should have replied: 'Sing on our show? You can't sing on any show!' I remember Eric showing me the letter and saying, 'Spike's quite right. It never crossed my mind.'

Spike and Eric would cross paths at the studios. I don't think that they particularly socialised together, but they clearly liked and admired each other. When Eric died, Spike was first up on breakfast TV talking about the sad loss, and what immense comic timing Eric possessed. Eric would have been very touched by that kindness.

Spike also reviewed Eric's first novel *Mr Lonely*, describing it as the best showbiz novel he'd ever read. Very kind, yet again.

Despite Eric's comedy being, for the most part, more mainstream than Spike's, they ironically approached their work in the same way. They were utterly professional and knew that if something was funny it was funny. You shouldn't analyse it. Just use it to make people laugh. It is interesting to note that Spike, like Eric, could appear on stage and say nothing, yet the audience would start falling about laughing. That is a truly great gift which only the chosen few – like Spike, like Eric, like Tommy Cooper, like Les Dawson – are given.

Many people would consider that the comedy of Morecambe and Wise is totally at odds with the comedy of Spike Milligan. But this is not so. Accepting that, to use the cliché, Spike's comedy is off the wall, how can that equate to the comedy of Morecambe and Wise? Well, if you consider two middle-aged men sharing a double bed, one writing a play while the other reads the *Dandy* and smokes a pipe, both pausing to discuss who 'teacher' liked best at school fifty years ago, or which of them had the best pair of shoes, you can start to appreciate that Eric and Ernie could also be off the wall in a very Spike Milligan way.

DR VINCENT SERVENTY

The President of the Wildlife Preservation Society of Australia recalls his time with Spike. This piece includes extracts taken from Vincent Serventy's autobiography, An Australian Life.

In Australia, only once did I spend a weekend with Spike when he was depressed, the rest of the time his environmental enthusiasm helped me in the fight for that great cause. Australia he appeared to enjoy. We loved him, as besides being a comic genius, he was a dedicated conservationist. He organised two free concerts for our society, the oldest in Australia and possibly the second oldest in the world. He arrived at the museum with four musicians and began by looking at me, standing in the rear. He said, 'Well, Vin, you talked me into this. What do you want me to do?' I was stunned but after a moment some inspiration came, I made some suggestion and he began. He kept the audience enthralled for two hours and many who were there have told me it was their most memorable theatre experience.

Spike often mentioned Woy Woy in his BBC shows. His mother lived there and he came often to see her and to work on his father's letters but he preferred to sleep in the quiet of our Creek Cottage. Sometimes he came alone, sometimes with his wife Shelagh. Once he asked in a note: 'What is that sweet smelling plant at your door? It always greets me with wild bush perfume – it's lovely when I arrive late at night to have a bush Cleopatra cloy me so.' It is a scented mint bush and when anyone walks in or out they brush against it. There is also a large lemon-scented ironwood nearby that releases an even stronger scent if its leaves are bruised.

On a bookshelf was a stone axe head I had found on the beach. Spike left another note: 'I saw your stone axe head. Still a workable tool after 200 years. I wonder where lies the Aboriginal who made it – his little axe lasted out his time. Will we?'

I told Spike how the World Wildlife Fund had funded a search for the long-lost Tasmanian tiger. I had played a major part in this decision, not because I thought we would find any live animals, but because the searching would provide information on a lot of others. Spike was scornful, regarding it as a waste of money, and left this poem:

> Have you seen the thylacine
> Or remotely where it's been
> People tell me by the score
> They have seen the creature's spoor
>
> It used to live here in Tasmania
> I'm certain no more remain there
> The thylacine is surely linked
> With other creatures now extinct.

> The poet of Woy Woy. Love, light and peace. Spike.

It was always fun and games with Spike; good dinners, good conversation and good wines.

JOHN CLEESE

One of the most significant talents in British comedy, renowned in particular for his roles as Python and Torquay hotelier Basil Fawlty, the actor and writer John Cleese describes Milligan's influence on him.

When people talk now about the revolution which transformed Britain in the 1960s, they think of the 'Angry Young Men' and the Beatles. For me, *The Goon Show* was much more subversive than *Look Back in Anger* – and Spike Milligan was the genius responsible for it.

It was a time when people were getting fed up with the stuffiness of England and asking: surely this can't be what life is all about? Writers like John Osborne and John Braine dealt with it through fury. The difference is that the Goons challenged the stuffiness with joy. They created a sense of liberation which went beyond laughter, evoking a strange, insane energy from people who suddenly found themselves breaking through the glass ceiling of respectability that had haunted them all their lives.

I knew Spike off and on for 35 years. But my first memory of him is as a teenager in the mid-1950s listening to *The Goon Show* on the radio, and being absolutely amazed by its surreal humour. It came at a key stage in my own development and I never missed a show. I remember triumphantly entering my living room, holding a copy of *Punch*, which my Dad thought was the bee's knees, and pointing to a good review of *The Goon Show* when they had done a parody of *Nineteen Eighty Four*, and saying 'You see, Dad – there are other people who like it.' Because, of course, my father thought the Goons were rubbish.

Spike, Peter Sellers and Harry Secombe were doing something that was at the same time very funny and very exhilarating. In comedy, there are a very small number of defining moments when somebody comes along and genuinely creates a breakthrough, takes us all into territory where nobody has been before. The only experiences to which I can compare my own discovery of the Goons are going to see N F Simpson's play *One Way Pendulum* at the Bristol Old Vic or, later on, hearing Peter Cook for the first time. They were just light-years ahead of everyone else.

In the 1950s, all the other performers were doing perfectly standard, sometimes quite decent, comedy, full of doors opening, and people coming in with catch phrases. Spike threw all that out. In Peter he had the best voice man in the world, and in Harry the wonderful innocent, who played the central role – it was on Harry's little adventure that each episode of *The Goon Show* took you. But Spike was the scriptwriter: it was he who invented Bluebottle, Minnie Bannister, Eccles and all the other great characters.

His influence on British comedy was, of course, enormous. We all loved *The Goon Show* in the Monty Python team: it ignited some energy in us. It was more a spirit that was passed on, rather than any particular technique. The point is that once somebody has crossed a barrier and done something that has never been done before, it is terribly easy for everybody else to cross it. In the late 1960s, there was a televised *Goon Show* and I was asked to pretend to be Wallace Greenslade, who had been the announcer on the radio show. I remember standing with the script, not quite believing it was happening. It was astounding. I felt I shouldn't be there but at the same time delighted that I was.

When we were filming *Monty Python's Life of Brian* in Tunisia in 1978, we discovered that Spike was there on holiday and asked him to appear in the movie. Typical Spike: he came along, was very friendly and very cheerful, and shot the scene in the morning. Then in the afternoon, after he had had lunch with us, and we went out to shoot the rest of the scene, he had gone. So we had to improvise. Still, we hadn't missed the opportunity to let him know that he had got us started, and had led the way. His unplanned appearance in that film was our homage to him.

Spike filming Life of Brian *on location in Tunisia.*
S.M. Collection

Where did it come from? For a start, Spike was a very British comedian. The fact is that, as much as one may like the continent of Europe in all other ways, there doesn't seem to be a tremendous amount of wonderful comedy coming out of there. But with the British, even in the stuffiest periods, there have been outbreaks of humour and insanity. In its strange restrained way, there is part of the British personality which relishes surrealism. Spike was like that: I remember him as somebody who wasn't particularly comfortable with emotion, so if you paid him a compliment he would probably make a joke and change the subject.

He was also drawing on a well-established tradition. Edith Sitwell would have loved Spike (although he was strictly speaking a British-Irish eccentric, rather than the English variety she wrote about). There are moments in Laurence Sterne and in Stephen Leacock's *Nonsense Novels* – which I know was an influence on Spike – where you get the same kind of insanity. He was the true inheritor of a kind of humour which you see in Edward Lear and Lewis Caroll. He took that highly intelligent genre and just ran with it in a way that nobody had ever run with it before.

He was the very bright working-class boy who went into the Army, saw it all from the inside – and knew exactly what a load of old cobblers it all was. *The Goon Show* was comedy but it was also a challenge to the whole social order. It was the very clever NCOs making jokes about the officers that the officers wouldn't quite have understood. Spike and the others were always slipping rude names and words past the BBC censors, who had no idea what was going on. For instance, they knew about cockney rhyming slang and what Hampton Wick was slang for. So there would be a character on the show called Sir Huge Hampton. And the BBC authorities never guessed.

There was a stupid class structure which needed to be kicked over. And with the Goons it wasn't done viciously but with joy. Spike opened the gate to a field of colourful, high-spirited comedy where nobody had been before. The sad thing is that I don't think he would be able to do it today, in an age when broadcasting is dominated by focus-group-oriented executives, people who think you can make great programmes by measuring things which can't actually be measured. That's the thing about Spike: you couldn't have designed him from scratch.

The above is a transcription of a telephone interview with Matthew D'Ancona of the *Telegraph*.

Moriarty

Minnie Bannister

S ← → N.

left, Spike dressed as Hitler for The Big Freeze *in Finland (c. 1992).*

MICHAEL PALIN

A key member of the legendary Monty Python team, Michael has recently been delighting television veiwers with his journeys around the world, about which he has also written bestselling books.

I first came across Spike Milligan in the mid-1950s, when I was twelve, listening to the revelatory radio series that was the Goons. Spike was both actor and writer, and I couldn't imagine what sort of person came up with these wonderfully rich, inventive scenarios every single week.

The importance of the Goons was that it was my own generation's programme and taste. My parents didn't know what was going on when they heard Henry and Minnie Crun, Eccles and all these strange voices. I think my father thought the wireless was broken, that one of the valves had gone. It was delicious to enjoy it myself, without the embarrassment of listening to it with my parents. Until then my experience of radio comedy had been through shared programmes such as *Much Binding in the Marsh* and *Take It From Here,* so this was a quantum leap and I thought it was extraordinarily exciting.

In my first term at Oxford I became close friends with Robert Hewison and one of the things we had in common was a shared love of the Goons and of Spike's work. There was an album he had produced called *Milligan Preserved*, which had a picture taken by Angus McBean of Spike's head in a jar. We thought that was wonderful. Inevitably, when I began writing my first comedy material at Oxford, I was greatly influenced by what he was writing.

Terry Jones and I adored the Q shows, which preceded *Python*. They were filled with surrealism and invention, and he took huge risks. He was the first writer to play with the conventions of television – having all his characters wear their costume name tags on screen, and captions to show the take-home pay of each actor as they appeared. It was glorious stuff. He played with the medium – sending up presenters or leaving gaps in the programme – just as he had in *The Goon Show*.

I liked the characters he built up, the cheek and audacity of his jokes, the fact that there were completely surreal moments, with no connection between one thought and the next. When it came to *Python*, Terry Jones and I were so impressed that we looked for the name of the director on the end of Q4 and hired him. That's how we met Ian MacNaughton, Spike's director who became the *Python* director.

I met Spike on several occasions at the BBC and got to know him quite well, though he was always rather a god-like figure. We all admired him greatly and used to go out after *Python* transmissions and have a meal together. Quite by chance, Spike was taking a holiday in Monastir in Tunisia when we were filming *The Life of Brian*, so he got to this hotel full not only of a film crew but the Pythons too. We put him in the film and he was brilliant as the man who finds Brian's shoe and gets trampled on – it was a vintage Spike performance, though I can remember him being slightly testy about the number of takes it needed to shoot the scene. He was on holiday after all.

About a year previously, Spike had sent me a very nice note about the *Ripping Yarns* series that I wrote with Terry Jones, written in his wonderfully stringy, looping script, saying how much he had enjoyed it. We were out at dinner in Monastir one night and Spike was regaling the gathering with the joy of *Ripping Yarns*. He proceeded to describe one of the stories, but it was completely as told by Spike and bore little relation to the characters I had written. Instead, he bounced off the characters with wild improvisations of his own.

I never wrote with him – Spike was from a different generation and we were all rather hierarchical in those days – and it would in any case have been quite tricky. He was a wild card and you were never quite sure what he would do. You could never pin him down and that was the essence of his comedy. He liked aiming the cannon at people, and if he felt upset about something he would really go for it. He wanted to have a free hand and to do things his own way. There would have been easier ways to write the *Goon Show*s, but he insisted on writing the whole lot himself even though it gave him a nervous breakdown. It was more important to him to work that way, and thus preserve his individuality and independence, than to compromise and become a paler version of Spike Milligan. To his credit, he never did do that. There is very little of Spike's work that is easy, conventional or blandly acceptable. It's all *Spiky*.

His film *The Running, Jumping & Standing Still Film* (1959) was way ahead of its time and encouraged a lot of us who wanted to make films in that surreal vein. That will be remembered, as will his books. The latter were never consistent, but they had some brilliant jokes and turns of phrase, and some genuinely moving reminiscences of the war. There was a side of Spike that was poetic, and he was rather a good poet. One of my particular favourites went:

> The boy stood on the burning deck
> Whence all but he had fled
> Twit.

His children's books were popular – my own children's favourite was *Badjelly the Witch*.

Though Spike had a very successful career, he regretted not having more television exposure after the Q shows. He was never ignored, but there was a feeling in Spike that the powers-that-be never really appreciated him. Yet that was one of the sources of his energy – a feeling close to paranoia. There was an obsessiveness in his work: he wrote intensely and things had to come from deep within him. The heart of Spike was in everything he wrote.

He campaigned for causes such as the environment and animal rights, and almost felt an identity with the animals and trees he fought for. He had an earthy, strong, spiritual quality and would never back down. That sometimes made him look a bit foolish, but the brilliant thing about him was that he could make a joke about anything, take on anybody.

On the TV show to celebrate his eightieth birthday, the presenter was talking about him and you suddenly heard his voice from behind the set – 'Shut up and get on with it'. It was Spike. Even at the age of eighty, he was sending things up, and refusing to lie down and be conformist.

BILL NUNN

For many years Bill was a stalwart of The Goon Show Preservation Society. His admiration for Spike turned into a friendship, which his mother shared.

I've liked Spike for quite a few years now, since I was about sixteen. When my brother was moving out of our home, he gave me one of his books. It was a paperback of *A Dustbin of Milligan* and I read it and enjoyed it. Shortly after that Mum bought me a tape recorder for Christmas and we went out to buy some tapes and I saw some *Goon Shows*. Mum asked, 'What are they?' I said, 'I don't know but Spike Milligan's in them so they must be good.' I played my very first *Goon Show* and, of course, I got hooked.

About three years later, when I bought *The Goon Show Companion* I discovered the address of The Goon Show Preservation Society and I wrote and joined up. Over the years, I progressed from printing back numbers of the newsletters, to actually helping with producing the new ones. Mum would put them in the envelopes and I would address them and put on the stamps to send out. I then ran the society shop for a number of years and most recently I was GSPS treasurer for a while.

Around 1975, when Spike was on television with the Q shows, I was always working late and missed them but when I got home, Mum would tell all about the show she'd watched. One day I said to her, 'I thought you didn't like Spike and you thought he was mad?' She replied, 'Well, he is but there was nothing else on.' So, I thought maybe she actually had a secret liking for him and found him funny. Consequently, I wrote to him, explaining what she did and asking for a signed photo. He very kindly sent one for her, signed, 'For Rose, love Spike Milligan.'

Some years later, when an opportunity arose for us to go and see one of his shows, *There's a Lot of It About*, with the GSPS, I asked for two tickets and took Mum along. We sat in the middle of the front row. Presently, there was an announcement and on came Spike. I'll never forget, he was wearing a denim shirt and jeans and Mum looked him up and down in this outfit. He asked, 'Hands up all those who like my humour,' and all the hands went up in the audience . . . except Mum's. So, he said, 'Right, hands up all those who don't like my humour.' Of course, I immediately nudged Mum and said, 'Go on, put your hand up; you don't like him.' So, Mum, slowly but surely, put her hand up. As Spike saw Mum sitting there all alone in the audience, with one hand up, he exclaimed, 'Ah, at last, an honest woman.'

He came to the front of the stage and continued, 'You don't like my humour?' Mum just stared at him, so he asked, 'Do you like Benny Hill?' And she replied that she did. Spike just turned away and walked off. Well, Mum was very upset; she thought she'd offended him.

After we had watched the first part of the show, Spike came back on and started talking about the old days. He said that they were the best days and there was a sort of murmur of agreement. Then he repeated himself and stared straight at Mum. She agreed enthusiastically and was delighted he'd spoken to her again. As the lights dimmed for the second show Spike accidentally walked into a closed door and shouted out, 'I've just walked into the bloody door . . . that was a Benny Hill joke!' And there was a roar of laughter.

At the end of the second show and the evening, Spike came on for the last time and thanked everyone for coming. He stopped in front of Mum and said, 'I'm sorry you like Benny Hill better than me.' She responded, 'No, Spike, I don't – I like you.' Whereupon he took both her hands and said, 'Have a safe journey home, God bless you, long life and happiness.'

We left the theatre and went into the foyer, where we stood chatting with another GSPS member and friend, Adrian Briggs. He'd been taking photos earlier in the day but had taken care to leave one shot, just in case he could photograph Mum and Spike together. With that, Spike came through the door to tell the audience that the BBC wouldn't allow a reception and to apologise. He saw Mum standing there and said, 'In any case, she likes Benny Hill better than me.' Mum was quick to deny it and I explained that she was worried she'd upset him. 'Of course she hasn't upset me. I asked an honest question and she gave an honest answer.'

When I asked if she could have her photo taken with him, he agreed immediately. As she posed there with him, he had his arm round her and said to me, 'Come on, you as well, you nana,' and I stood the other side of him.

As you can see in the photo, Mum was wearing a dress, which had a piece of material that could be used as a belt or a bow round the neck. She took this off the dress and Spike signed his name on it for her. Well, this is the only item of her clothing I've kept since she died seven years ago and it's been washed many, many times but his name has never worn off. People would remark on it to her when she wore it. Even today, you can still clearly see 'Spike Milligan' on it and I continue to treasure it, just as she did.

After that, whenever we went to his shows, nine times out of ten, when Spike heard that there was a lady with a walking stick to see him, Mum and I would go into his dressing room for a chat. On one occasion, we were waiting outside the Lyric Theatre for a taxi when the security man asked us to go inside. Spike was sitting on the stairs. I said hello to him, adding, 'I don't think you remember my mum.' He replied, 'Of course I remember her, otherwise I wouldn't have come out to say hello and ask how she is.'

We always received Christmas cards from Spike and Shelagh every year. We got them a wedding present when they married and Spike wrote to say thank you.

Mum grew very fond of Spike and her revised view was, 'I still think he's mad but in an ingenious way.' Those meetings were very special to her and to me.

Spike with Bill Nunn and his mother.

LYNSEY DE PAUL

The singer and composer Lynsey de Paul's affectionate friendship with Spike began over twenty years ago. I grew up listening to the Goons on the radio. When I was five or six years old I would walk around my house putting on a silly voice, saying, 'He's fallen in the water'. The Goons made an impact on little girls, the general public, and influenced comedy teams for generations thereafter.

I met Spike in 1980 when I accompanied James Coburn to the *Parkinson* show, where both were appearing as guests. An enduring friendship started that night.

Spike nicknamed me 'Loony de Small' and called me a cross between Alice in Wonderland and a storm trooper. I nicknamed him 'Shtick Milliner', as he was a comic genius and could be mad as a hatter.

Spike was one of those people that filled any room, TV, film screen or theatre with his presence. He had the speediest wit and a completely original way of expressing humour. Once, when I was staying for the weekend at his home by the coast, the phone rang for me. I was concerned that Spike thought that people knew it was his phone number.

'It's OK, Spike,' I said, 'no one knows where I am.'

'Do you know where you are?' he replied.

'Leave me alone,' I laughed.

To which he said: 'I'd like a loan too!'

Despite his silliness, Spike was consummately compassionate, and concerned about the planet and animal protection. Like me, he was a vegetarian. On one occasion, he coerced me into demonstrating outside the Australian Embassy against the redirection of a Tasmanian dam, which would have resulted in the killing of thousands of animals. I dressed sombrely for the demonstration, while he turned up wearing a large broad-rimmed hat strewn with dozens of corks on string and with a guitar hung about his neck.

As most people knew, he was a man of extremes. He would be hysterically funny but manically depressed; compassionate but intolerant; loving but critical. I remember him being like an ecstatic child eagerly anticipating a new bike when, after undergoing a triple heart-bypass and despite other health problems, he carefully organised a parachute jump for his eightieth birthday; thankfully his doctor managed to dissuade him. However, when suffering from depression, he could be unreasonable and unapproachable. He called me to complain that he could not find the tea in his kitchen. 'I can't find the tea,' he yelled down the phone. 'What's the point of having a wife if you can't find the tea in your own kitchen?' And he meant it. His wife, Shelagh, was a saint, and, in fact, Spike loved her very much and could not have survived without her.

Spike would invite me to his legendary one-man West End shows, put me in a front row seat and then, at the end of his show (to my horror), insist that I come up on stage to sing a song. I used to dread going on stage 'cold' when the audience had paid to see *him* and he had been making everyone, including the ushers, cry with laughter. One night I was invited to his show at the Lyric in London's Shaftsbury Avenue, and I knew that not only was the Welsh Guard attending, but that, secretly, Prince Charles would be there. Now Spike Milligan was a hard act to follow for anyone at any time, so, just in case, I wrote a song especially for the occasion called 'Forgettable', which was a pastiche on the song 'Unforgettable'. The end of the show came and Spike pointed a finger at me, directing me on the stage. My heart began pounding, and, as Spike knew I was a shy performer, he sat right at the end of the piano for the whole song with a smile on his face. I felt better. The audience was expecting a serious composition, but by the second verse they started to laugh. That was one of those special moments in a life, which you re-run on your 'mental DVD' over and over again.

Apart from being a comedy mastermind and very musical, Spike was well educated. His conversation was peppered with broad reference, and he had extraordinary recall. I watched him play the piano, the trumpet and the guitar with varying degrees of competence but with equal enthusiasm, and he loved composing songs. To my astonishment, he wrote a song about me, and sang it to me one day while playing the piano. I was profoundly moved.

A SONG FOR LYNSEY DE PAUL
'BEING YOU' (February 1987) Spike Milligan

Being you – what's it like just being you
In a mirror seeing you
Can you turn away?
Such a face
Like a fire in outer space
All the grace and the pace
Of a Cleopatra – Turbo Mantra
What to do

When you meet somebody who
Puts some kind of spell on you
Goes and rings the bell on you
It's hell on you.
So you just stand and wait
Like a beggar at the palace gate
Waiting for that cruel Medusa glance
A smile perchance
The eyes, the lips, the spell, the trance
I wish I knew – just what it's like
Being you.

His originality, humour, poems and books have given us all a magical legacy. He wrote a dedication for me in one of those books. It read: 'In the human race today – you came last!' For me, Spike, wherever you are, in the human race -– you came first.

Spike and Lynsey de Paul after the West End opening of his one-man show.

GYLES BRANDRETH

The writer, broadcaster and former MP recalls an evening of Milligan nonsense. Some twenty years ago I edited an anthology of nonsense verse to which Spike Milligan kindly contributed both some inimitable gems and an appropriately lunatic introduction. For the launch of the book a special reading of nonsense verse was organised at the Poetry Society in Earls Court Square, with Spike himself billed as the star attraction.

The evening was quite informal. Guests were supplied with warm white wine and invited to sit on upright chairs facing an improvised stage. In the middle of the stage was a large wooden crate covered with a checked tablecloth (1950s French bistro style) on which the readers of the verse placed their wine glasses, ashtrays and copies of the book.

I was to be master of ceremonies and felt reasonably comfortable about the event because little was required of me and I knew that the audience was not coming to see or hear me, but coming to relish the unique genius of Spike. Unfortunately as I arrived at the Poetry Society, I found a message waiting for me: 'Mr Milligan has been delayed. He will hope to be with you shortly.' We waited and waited. A further message came: 'Mr Milligan has been further delayed.' We had no alternative but to start the poetry reading. The audience was clearly disappointed, but they coped with what I and the other performers who had gathered were offering, consoled by the prospect of Spike arriving shortly. The interval came: still no sign of the master. During the interval, a final telephone message arrived: 'Mr Milligan has gone to heaven. He very much regrets that he cannot be with you after all.'

As the audience shuffled back to their seats for the second half of the evening, I called for hush and read out the disappointing news. As what I had to tell them was received with a mixture of sighs and heavy groans, something quite extraordinary happened. The lid of the crate on the stage began to move. The glasses and the ashtrays and the books slithered and crashed to the floor. The lid was pushed back and out stepped the matchless Milligan to rapturous – no, riotous – applause. He had been hidden in that box for at least two hours.

*'*The sun comes up on time, so why can't we?*'*

- On being a stickler for punctuality

CHRIS OWER

Chris runs College Farm (one of London's farms) in Finchley. Whenever the farm ran into trouble, he was able to count on the help and support of Spike.

It was about 1982 that Spike first came over to College Farm. He was president of the Finchley Society, which he had founded with Jean Scott, and she asked him to come down. However, strangely enough, I had met him before that when I worked for the BBC at White City. The first show I helped on was Q – it was hilarious. Things did go wrong but they were still funny! I remember there was a scene where there was a séance round a table and someone had to say, 'Knock if there's anyone there', and Spike was supposed to burst through the wall. What he didn't know was that it had been covered with heavily embossed wallpaper; so, he rushed at the wall but bounced straight off. I was told to sort it out and I got a knife and loosened the paper but nobody told Spike. So, the next time he took even more of a run at the wall, hit it, came straight through, went over the table and ended up in front of the audience!

After that I was called to see the head of the department and naturally I was worried because I thought I was going to be told off. But I wasn't, he said he'd like to read a letter to me from the producer congratulating me on my work on the show and he gave me a £50 bonus. When I told my colleagues, they called me all sorts of names!

So, in 1982, it wasn't the first time I had met Spike but, of course, he couldn't remember me on Q, as there were so many people involved in it over all the years. He came and looked around the farm and then contacted ITV's news team. They filmed all the dilapidation and it created quite a lot of interest. Spike also wrote to the Department of Transport, which was the ministry that owned the farm in those days, and wrote regularly to Mrs Thatcher. I'm sure they became pen pals over the years he corresponded with her about College Farm! The Ministry of Transport had given us notice to quit and Spike helped to have that quashed.

One day, my family and Spike were sitting in an empty room when Spike suddenly started scraping the wall. He asked me for a knife and I handed one over. It turned out Spike had discovered there were Minton tiles there, over one hundred years old, and historians later verified them. That was one of the reasons we were able to get the farm buildings listed. Sue Russell restored the room and we opened it as a tea room with her running it; it won 'The Best Tea House' for five years.

In those days, we not only had the farm but also kept horses, offered horse-riding lessons and manufactured horse feed. But in 1985, with high inflation and people not paying for their feed, we fell into financial trouble. On top of this, part of the main building had collapsed. The Ministry of Transport told me I had to pay for the repairs myself. This would have cost £20,000 and it looked like we would go bankrupt. Spike, however, got *That's Life* interested in us. He even took a calf on the show; we still have that cow! Spike told Paul Getty to watch the programme and he and the Wellcome Foundation both donated enough to pay off our debts.

After *That's Life,* interest in the farm really took off and I would often have two phones ringing at once. Once when I was on both of them at the same time a man came up and threw money through the window, saying, 'Keep fighting! Good luck!'

Spike was often funny on the phone, he'd answer it and say, 'This is not an answer phone – this is me!' Once, when I had to see Spike, I'd just had a tooth out and I went directly from the dentist's to Spike's house. I was told he was in his room, so I went up to find him sitting up in bed, on the phone. He took one look at me and said into the receiver, 'There's someone here with a fat face, who wants to try and speak to me!'

One day, Spike turned up and asked, 'Have you got a good contact at the Ministry of Transport?' I replied that I had and he asked me to telephone him. I told the man that I had Spike Milligan with me and that Spike wanted to speak with him, but he thought I was joking. Anyway, I handed over the telephone and Spike announced, 'I have a cheque here for £1 million, will you sell me the farm?' Unfortunately, the answer was no. That was a bad decision and they've made a loss since then.

In 1996, the ministry decided the farm was surplus to requirements. We set up a trust to buy the farm and Spike agreed to be patron. It was settled that whatever the highest bid was, we would match it and the ministry would sell it to us. As there was no definite target, we had to tell people we would give back any donations over £50 and ask for pledges instead. It was a logistical nightmare.

In October 2001, a price was finally agreed. It took six months to obtain the sale agreement from the government's solicitors and when we did get it, there were conditions stating we cannot use lottery money or private funding. So, we are back to square one. I'm still fighting on and the trustees have agreed to a new farm centre, which would be dedicated to Spike.

All this takes me back to when the researchers came from *That's Life* and spent three hours with Spike and me, going into everything and talking about the problems. After the meeting, I thanked Spike for everything and he replied, 'Don't thank me, I'm just a cowboy.' I wasn't sure what he meant by that and I said that he knew, as everyone did, that we had to save the farm. His reaction was, '**** the farm, let's save you and Jane!'

Everyone else was busy saving the farm but Spike was fighting for us, and all the time the lovely Shelagh has been there for us as well. Spike knew what we were up against; we were (and still are) up against bureaucracy. You can see Spike's mind working: he sees through a problem, whereas others go round it. We've always kept in touch but I haven't rung him lately because I only want to give him good news. However, we will be forever in his debt; if it hadn't been for him, we wouldn't be here today, so I always say Spike saved College Farm. I feel very privileged to know the other side of Spike, the side others don't know. Really, he's too intelligent for his own good.

*'*The people of Greenpeace are my heroes. The governments are trying to save the lifestyle that they've always known. But Greenpeace are trying to save the world.*'*

ED WELCH

A successful composer who worked with Spike, Ed has very kindly given permission for extracts to be taken from his unpublished notebooks, **Joseph – I'm Having a Baby:** **A Diary of a Good Idea.**

'I've got an idea for a clown's Nativity,' said Spike. Before I had a chance to ask him how he'd define a clown's Nativity, he whipped in with the title: 'We'll call it *Joseph – I'm Having a Baby.*'

I can remember being completely bowled over by that title. We were having dinner down in a South Kensington restaurant in winter 1977, and I'm afraid that whatever cuisine I was enjoying at the time left my mouth as if shot from a gun, unfortunately in the direction of Paddy Milligan, Spike's late wife.

I had met Spike some three or four years before. At the time I was 26, working as a music publisher's assistant. I was particularly involved with film music and its promotion and I was longing for a chance to write some film music myself.

One particular sheet of music that found its way on to my desk was the main theme from a Michael Caine film, *Loot*. The music was by George Martin and there appeared to be a lyric sheet attached. To my amazement and joy, this was in what I now know as the distinctive hand of Spike Milligan. I suppose, like many others, I had long been a fan of Spike's, I'd held him in awe. I was surprised to see him writing lyrics for film themes, although it's not far from his skill of writing poetry.

With an eye for the main chance, I opened my desk and drew out a cassette of a tune I had just written. By good fortune I had been able to include this tune on a large orchestral session I was conducting, so it sounded very 'Hollywood'. I popped it, and a suitable letter, into an envelope, gleaned Spike's address out of the copyright department and dispatched it hopefully in the direction of Bayswater.

Spike, Ed Welch and Virginia Gallico at the recording of The Snow Goose *in August 1977.*

Here it was to lie for a good few weeks yet. In fact, I had forgotten entirely about it when the phone rang on my desk. 'Have you heard about the Irishman awaiting execution and there's something wrong with the guillotine?' I was at once aware who my caller was and, as often happened, was lost for words. Spike thanked me profusely for troubling to send him a tune, apologised for not phoning earlier but explained he had been in

Cyprus making a TV advert. He went on to say that he hadn't listened to the tune yet but intended to as soon as the call was over. I was arrogant enough to think he'd like it, so I sat quietly at the desk until the phone rang about ten minutes later. The tone was altogether different:

'Did *you* write this?' he asked, very quietly and sincerely.

'Yes,' I replied.

'Well, I'm cancelling everything for the next few days to write a lyric.'

And he did!

A few days later Spike emerged from his darkened office and read to me over the phone the most exquisite lyric it is possible to imagine. Called 'Did It Happen?', it can be read in his collection of poems, *Open Heart University*. I quickly made a demonstration recording with a female singer and before very long we had eight excellent recordings of the song.

It was time the composer and author met each other and, shortly after doing the demo record, Spike invited me to his office. As I knocked and entered with some temerity, he didn't raise his eyes from the desk but sat finishing off some work or other. He told me to sit on the couch and keep taking the pills. Eventually, he looked up and seemed to gasp. It appeared that he had been expecting someone rather older and less 'way out'. He seemed pleased anyway and it was my impression that we got on very well.

That was how we met and over the next year or so he made a great effort to involve me in any musical project he could. I appeared as guest singer on his Christmas TV show, *The Last Turkey in the Shop Show*. I also set to music his book, *Badjelly the Witch*, and we collaborated on a musical setting of *The Snow Goose*. Further TV appearances followed. Spike is a very musical man although he finds the *business* of music a depressing affair.

It was late 1977 when Spike mentioned *Joseph – I'm Having a Baby* and over the following weeks it began to dawn on me that nothing was going to happen. Perhaps Spike had had a brainstorm, thought up a title and decided to ditch it. He kept saying he'd do it one day but at the same time postponed any starting date, citing quite reasonably his diary, which was crammed to bursting with commitments.

A year later, I moved to Devon but I still thought of the project in idle moments. A few months before Christmas 1980 I took up my script again and phoned Spike with a vengeance. We must do it, I pleaded, it wouldn't take that long and if we put time in *now* we'd be ready for Christmas 1981.

His continual insistence was that if this show were to be done, it must be excellent. For too long, he complained, he had taken the money and run. Not since *The Goon Show* had he been pleased with what he had done. When one considers the joys of *Puckoon* and *Adolf Hitler, My Part in his Downfall*, one is a little mystified. However, I at least began to feel he was realising that it *could* be written.

Spike's reluctance stemmed from the enormity of the task, coupled with a desire to get it right. Another factor was his domestic life. Since the death of Paddy, Spike had been bringing up his daughter Jane and to an extent, Silé. He had a large house with staff and just the same domestic and mundane problems as everybody else. These domestic chores and expenses meant that Spike had to do a good deal of lucrative contract work to keep the whole operation on the go. Around March 1981, about four years after our initial dinner when Spike suggested the title, I really began to feel we were creating something.

9–20 March 1981

Spike has been hard at his lyrics, we seem to speak every day on the phone. We've got eight songs ready now, at least on paper. Some of Spike's lyrics are really excellent, though, as usual, he is not satisfied. One title that has bothered him is 'Don't Be A Man Too Soon'. This is a song I see Mary singing to baby Jesus. Spike has written a great couplet:

> Don't butterfly too soon
> You're safer, so much safer, a cocoon.

That is Spike at his best. He is worried by the word 'man'. As he put it, the audience will expect baby Jesus to put on his hat and go out for a f***ing walk! However, he realises that 'Don't Be A Man Too Soon' sings well and so, for the moment, that stays.

6–7 April 1981

We record the demos. The big question mark is – what sort of frame of mind will he be in? Contrary to usual belief, Spike is very easy to work with, a real pro. He doesn't suffer fools gladly and I've made sure there are no fools around today. I needn't have worried, he was in splendid form – helpful, creative and funny.

8 April 1981

Vast confusion as Spike and I and the engineer all try and book taxis for the tape to get to Lord Delfont's office. Spike is in a foul mood – still with laryngitis from the first day's efforts and really pissed off with the world. He wants to know if the taxi has delivered the tape. I'm in Devon by now so haven't a clue. He phones Lord Delfont's office and asks the young secretary if she is 'Secretary number 1045?' I suppose people put up with this because it's Spike. Eventually, the tape does arrive, so now we'll have to sit and wait.

13 May 1981
I did some new tracks in Torquay to send to Spike for lyrics. I used, deliberately, some sound effects; Spike is mad on FX (and echoes as well). When we were doing *The Snow Goose*, he was all for borrowing a swan from Sir Peter Scott, putting a radio mike round its neck and recording the wing beat in flight. Needless to say, it didn't happen. On this project, he will *insist* that it does.

15 May 1981
Spike loved the Annunciation Song. He particularly loved the wind effect and wants to use this on stage, orchestrated and harmonised with the voice. Spike was very kind on the phone, saying lots of good things about my music. He really can be the nicest guy on the face of the earth. We all need praise, especially if you're a writer.

1 June 1981
Spike's due back from Australia next week. I miss our daily chat on the phone and, paradoxically, although it's me who does most of the driving on the show at this stage, when he's not there to bounce ideas off little gets done.

8 July 1981
For the first time in ages I am able to report progress on an artistic level. Spike has been quietly at work on the Annunciation Song. He sung to me over the phone the first working of his lyric, which shows fantastic promise. He described a choirboy interrupting Mary as she is doing a fairly mundane chore, touching her with his fingers and telling her she has been chosen. There was a lump in Spike's throat as he described it and I was overjoyed that we are back in action. He promised to work on it for the rest of the day.

24 July 1981
Spike phoned today at 9am, a usual time for him, and in good form. He's going for a fitting for his Royal Wedding suit today, so he explained that he wouldn't be writing much. The choreography now

looks to be in favour of Paddy Stone. He also told me that Alan Clare, the pianist, had picked up my Shillingbury Tales theme by ear. 'Most people bend down and use their hands,' came the follow-up remark.

Altogether, these comments at nine in the morning give the reader an idea of how his brain works – as fast as lightning.

25 July 1981

Spike is getting paranoid about not being able to sleep – such is the traffic noise in London and thereabouts. Actually, he already has double-glazing in his bedroom and it is away from the traffic. Someone is going up this evening to give him an estimate for a complete padded-cell job. I imagine if he doesn't get a good night's sleep soon, that's exactly what they'll put him in. Living in Devon, we have to be careful not to be woken by seagulls and waves! I'm not going to invite him to stay here because I'd be terrified the dog might bark in the night.

3 August 1981

Spike is very concerned for my wellbeing, financially speaking, and would feel happier if he were to lend me money because of delays attributable to himself. I would rather not accept but I do appreciate his gestures.

Spike normally answers his phone promptly and tersely with the word 'Next!' This morning, when I phoned him, he answered, 'How to write a musical!' Then suggested I got off the line!

8 September 1981

Spike should be back from his holidays very soon, to get cracking on a certain project. When I spoke to him before he went, he sounded in the absolute pits. *No one* sounds as low as Spike when he's down, barely able to mumble a few words. No consolation seemed to help at all and I just stood with the phone to my ear feeling acutely embarrassed.

19 September 1981

Spike invited me to dinner at home on Tuesday, and I was humbled by the effort he and Shelagh went to, to make me feel welcome and well fed. I really feel part of the family now and that's very reassuring.

7 October 1981

I phoned Spike today, to find him in bed with manic depression. He begged me to have a chat and cheer him up. I did better than that, I played him my tune for 'I've Got Everything' – a duet we plan between Herod and Joseph early in the show. He was completely knocked out by it and I felt his spirits rise dramatically. 'Believe it or not,' he said, 'I'm a fan of yours!' It's difficult to set down in words this relationship we have. Geographically, age-wise and experience-wise we shouldn't really work together at all, apart say from me arranging some of his songs. I've worked in that capacity with many well-known people, better known than Spike in some ways, yet the best that's happened might be a drink in a bar after a session and that's it. I'm now known for my work with Spike and am constantly asked about how he is and what he's like to work with. I'm tired of explaining to people that I can't put it in a nutshell.

24 October 1981

Spike went to Africa on the 14th for some work and during the trip wrote a couple of scenes for the show. On his return, a day or so ago, he was pleased to report that he has now got into the character of Joseph – an essential (I imagine!) for any writer. We have now also finished another two songs of a comic variety. These are 'The Goat Song', that tells of the injustices of ending up as a drinking bottle hung on the wall when starting life as a goat's bladder! The other song, 'I've Got Everything', is a duet between Herod and Joseph on the lines of 'Anything You Can Do, I Can Do Better'. It is filled with delightful badinage like:

Herod: 'I've got money.'

Joseph: 'I've got piles!'

24 November 1981

Spike is in the pits of despair. It seems the show is only one hour forty minutes – not the two hours we need. Spike had prepared letters and envelopes to everybody to send copies of scripts – only to have to collect everything in and start to write an extra twenty minutes of show.

Imagine my feelings when after a mere fifteen seconds of telling me about the short length of the play, the phone went dead on me. Five minutes later the phone rang again and it was Spike, claiming he'd been talking to himself for a good three minutes, during which time he had explained the whole f***ing thing and wasn't going through it again for anybody. Only after I promised to cough every twenty seconds to reassure him he still had contact would he agree to explain it all again. The sun is shining in Devon but it must be very thundery over Barnet way!

8 December 1981

I am delighted to report that Spike has refinished the script. The effort involved in adding twenty minutes to a script but not altering anything must be colossal, yet he's done it and I'm mightily grateful. I'm going up to London tomorrow to stay at Spike's, partly to do a promo film with him for Television South West, and partly to go over the various reprises that will be required in the show.

12 December 1981

Spike just phoned (it's tea time on a cold Saturday afternoon) to literally blow his top about the excellence of the music. He simply couldn't get the words out fast enough and my ego went straight through the roof.

It seems that his daughters requested the demo tapes to be played while they decorated the Christmas tree. The songs 'Mary' and 'Dreaming' are absolute winners for Spike's money and, in his most confident mood yet, Spike told me what Richard Mills could do with himself if he didn't see the success of this show.

15 December 1981

Spike has delivered the script to Richard Mills today, by car. In all honesty, the next few days will decide whether I write any more diary, music, or anything else to do with the show. If Mr Richard Mills doesn't like the script then we can forget it. I'm worried – not because there's anything wrong with the script, or anything wrong with Richard . . . I'm just worried.

January 1982

Richard laid before us his plan: to put *Joseph* into a subsidised theatre such as Leicester, Bristol, the R.S.C. or National, to inject about £100,000 into *that* production and then, when and if the time is right, to bring it to the West End.

My initial reaction was acute disappointment – no West End opening – but slowly it dawned on me that we could have a much better and tighter show as a result of this move, although we might risk it never coming to the West End. I looked at Spike, whose reaction was a mixture of surprise and relief: 'Leicester – great, I can stay with my aunt!'

Sadly, *Joseph – I'm Having A Baby* never made it on to the stage but the tapes and script are still in the Milligan house . . . waiting.

PROFESSOR ANTHONY CLARE

Professor Clare has helped and influenced millions with his highly perceptive and popular radio programme, In the Psychiatrist's Chair, and also with the book he wrote with Spike.

When I interviewed Spike for *In the Psychiatrist's Chair* and the book we did together, *Depression and How to Survive It*, I could find no single cause for his illness. I know there was a family history of depression in Spike's background and he had persistent depressive tendencies; he was pre-disposed to it. I think the first cause was the rupture he experienced when the family moved from India to Lewisham in London. He had had a reasonably stable life in India and saw it as idyllic. London was a bitter disappointment to him, as I think many things have been since that time. Later, of course, came the war when he was blown up. He was invalided out because his sensitive personality meant he couldn't stand the noise and the chaos. Then later, in the early 1950s, the manic over-work took its toll and he had a breakdown. He was churning out scripts and couldn't cope with the stress of that and of battling to make everything perfect.

It's hard to imagine Spike as a comic genius without his sort of personality. Manics love wordplay; puns, rhymes and the bizarre association of ideas, all of which Spike was able to incorporate into scripts. Spike's ability to write his ideas and comedy into brilliant working scripts shows a rare degree of control, which is all bound up with his comic genius.

Of course, when Spike occasionally had pure depression he did put himself to bed and withdraw from life. But at the time of the Goons he seems to have been in a mixed effective state, which enabled him to keep on working through most of it. One of the interesting things about Spike is his enormous appetite for public approval. Audience reactions gave him a jolt – just like someone with a flat battery who experiences ECT.

As a result of his temperament and his past experiences, he has enormous anger: not so much now as he is more serene, but he's remained angry about his early childhood move to London and has felt taken for granted since then. He copes with these bad feelings by projecting out his anger. Spike became very miserable when I put to him that he behaved towards other people in a way he wouldn't tolerate in them. He sometimes blames them for something which is actually caused by some failing within himself, but instead of blaming himself he blames the other person. He does this because he won't admit he's not perfect – he couldn't bear that. So, sometimes, he bites the hand that feeds him and those closest to him suffer most.

However, Spike has suffered enormously through his life. He's experienced pain in his relationships and he's sensitive enough to suffer quite a bit because of it. His sensitivity is like having a layer of skin missing and he is very vulnerable to any adverse criticism. But, as I say, now he is more tranquil and I think that is due to the fact that, at last, he is beginning to be recognised for the genius that he undoubtedly is.

Spike, the man, is a maddening, demanding, engaging and irritating combination of self-confidence and sensitivity, of ego and single-mindedness but he is still a child. He never grew up; he stopped at about eleven when he came to England. It was so gloomy and disappointing to him that he wanted to remain the child he'd been in India. So, he kept his ability to think like a child, seeing the world in simplistic terms with this maddening innocence. I'm not patronising him when I say that he is a comic genius who remains a child at heart.

He has enormous appeal to people because, in a world with cloning qualities, where we use words like 'globalisation' and 'internationalisation', we are told to be like each other, eat the same things, watch the same things, like the same things, Milligan is a one-off, there really is nobody like him. We crave and adore difference and he is different. Whether people like him or not, everyone will have heard of Spike Milligan. In addition to which, of course, he has this extraordinary ability to make people laugh. Spike's best aspects are his great kindness and his huge desire to be loved. They are touching and no great fault.

I don't mind dying. I just don't want to be there when it happens.

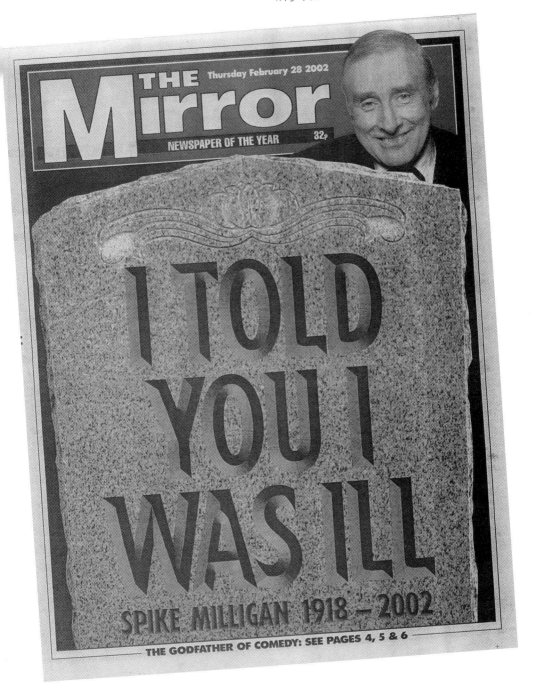

The Mirror *memorably announces Spike's death – Milligan fashion.*
Reproduced with the personal permission of the editor, Piers Morgan, whose
warm response was, 'Yes, of course, I'd be delighted if you did.'

SIRJOHN LAMBERT

Sir John worked for English Heritage for a number of years and, in this role, his path crossed Spike's with a mutually happy result.

I came to know and enjoy the friendship of Spike and Shelagh some years back through just one of Spike's many-sided interests. This concerned his involvement with his local 'Heritage' group in north London.

As Director of the Heritage of London Trust, I was working with English Heritage and the London boroughs, helping to restore and preserve some of the less widely known architectural treasures for the benefit of local communities and Londoners generally.

Between 1988 and 1992 I collaborated with Spike on one particular project of close interest to him. This concerned the Roman Catholic St Peter's Church, 103 Woolwich New Road, London. The church architect, whom I knew, was Mr T. Houlihan RIBA. It is an early church by the great Pugin (1843) with a later chancel, Grade II listed.

The church was in a struggling area and had, over the years, suffered from neglect. But in the 1980s the priest, Father Niall Thornton, had done some splendid work with his congregation of 500 and had somehow raised a substantial sum for basic repair work. However, a further £50,000 or so was still needed for major work and the church had applied for grant aid to English Heritage.

Spike had a special interest in this church, as his grandparents had married and his mother had been christened there. He therefore got on to me since he knew that the Heritage of London Trust, which I ran, worked closely with English Heritage on such projects.

After visiting the church in April 1989, I recommended to the Board of the Trust that we offer a grant of £7,500 to restore an important feature: the elaborate moulded doorway at the west bay of the south aisle. Our help would complement that of English Heritage on the rest of the church. This was duly agreed.

Spike undertook to do what he could to help, including obtaining useful publicity for the project. Meanwhile, I arranged with the architect for a plaque to be prepared for the church acknowledging the assistance of all concerned.

In April 1992, the plaque was duly unveiled with suitable ceremony by Spike and with the media in attendance. The upshot was that the *Sun* and *Mail on Sunday* each carried a short piece recording that Spike had wanted to save the church because of his family links and had enrolled my support, with successful results. The local *Woolwich and Charlton Mercury* of 9 April 1992 carried a jolly article, not quite accurate on financial detail but no matter! The Trust is still going strong after twenty years.

In collaborating with Spike in this field, we found that, as old soldiers, we had something else in common. We had both served in Tunisia with the British First Army (1942–43) and later in Italy (1944–45). We had a shared feeling that under the publicity-conscious 'Monty', the Eighth Army had stolen rather more than their fair share of the limelight in North Africa. After the war, the First Army had not even been represented at the annual Field of Remembrance ceremony at Westminster Abbey. Spike proceeded to rectify this omission a few years ago with the support of a group of friends and old comrades of whom I was proud to be one. I remember that one was Lord (Bernard) Miles, the actor, and that we all met for lunch under his auspices at the House of Lords.

The above two 'good causes', though just minor features of Spike's colourful and variegated life, represent matters which he felt to be important and worthwhile and are further reasons for us to feel admiration for this remarkable man of our times.

Before they left London, my wife and I enjoyed Spike and Shelagh's hospitality and they ours. Now we just correspond but the affectionate link remains. He really is so very special.

A miracle, by Goon!

FUNNYMAN Spike Milligan worked a little miracle in Woolwich last week.

The ex-Goon was on a pilgrimage to St Peter's RC church, Woolwich New Road, where his mother was christened and his grandparents were married, only to find the Victorian Gothic revival building was sadly in need of refurbishment.

It was designed by the eminent Victorian architect Augustus Welby Pugin, who also designed the Houses of Parliament and Southwark Cathedral.

Spike got straight on the phone to Sir John Lambert, director of the Heritage of London Trust, who is a friend of his.

Sir John, who until that moment had never heard of the church, came straight down to investigate — and the result was a £100,000 joint grant from the trust and from

by TRACY GAYTON

English Heritage.

Delighted parishioners, who had already raised £250,000 themselves, will now be able to complete restoration work.

Spike said: "When I visited the church, I realised it was a real little gem. But the priest there, Father Niall Thornton, was bemoaning the lack of funds to carry out all the work needed. So I was able to tip off the people who were actually able to help.

"It seems like a little miracle that the money was found during a recession and I'm very pleased about it.

"I've tried to do things before, like save ponds, and haven't always had a lot of luck. Seeing the church as it is today, makes me want to go down on my knees."

Spike's great-grandfather, his grandfather and his father were Woolwich-based Royal Artillery gunners. His grandparents were married at the church on March 5 1882 and his mother, Florence Mary Winifred Kettleband, was later baptised there.

● BLESS ME! Spike with Fr Thornton

Above, a local newspaper article about St Peter's Church, Woolwich New Road, which Spike campaigned for.

FIRESIGN THEATER

Firesign Theater has its home in the United States but its roots seem to have been planted in Milligan's Goon soil. The founding members explain –

David Ossman: We all listened to *The Goon Show* at various times in our lives. We heard a lot of those shows. They impressed us when we started doing radio ourselves, because they sustained characters in a really surreal and weird kind of situation for a long period of time. They were doing that show for ten years, all the way through the 1950s. So we were just listening to them at the end. It was that madness and the ability to go anywhere and do anything and yet sustain those funny characters. So when we first did written radio in 1967, when we would sit down and write half-hour skits and do them once a week, we did things that were very imitative of *The Goon Show* and learned a lot of voices from them.

Phil Proctor: I'm just a fan. I was introduced to them through the group and I loved them and that's just it. We loved the surrealism that was in the group so much that we got enthusiastic about it and did our performances in that style. It was just a part of our live performance from a *Goon Show* point of view. We did a lot of English-type characters so I would take inspiration from the Goon kind of wild, fast high-voiced approach to things. It was homage work.

Peter Bergman: When I was in England in 1965, I was writing for *Not So Much a Programme, More a Way of Life*, which was the antecedent to *That Was The Week That Was*. I went to see Spike Milligan who was performing in a play called *Oblomov*. He was improvising it so that basically it became his one-man show. I went backstage to say hello. I didn't know who these people were. I had no idea who the Goons were; I just thought Spike Milligan was marvellous. We made a great contact and decided to write together. We started to put together an article for *Queen* magazine. I don't know if the magazine still exists. So we spent some time together in London and it was really quite wonderful.

I have two Spike Milligan stories. One is that we were walking down the street once and we went by an undertaker's establishment. He walked in, there was nobody there in the front. He laid down on the counter, put his hands over his chest and yelled, 'Shop!'* The other time we went into a restaurant and we ordered a bottle of wine. As it came to the table he picked it up and yelled, 'Waiter, waiter! There's no ship in this bottle!' So it was wonderful working with him. He was a great genius.

Phil Austin: I've been a devotee of the Goons since I first heard them, in Fresno, in the 1950s, when they were played as part of an NBC Radio weekend programme called *Monitor*. When I went to work at KPFK, working my way up to drama and literature director, one of my jobs was to programme the *Goon Shows* from a huge library of transcription discs that KPFK had received from the BBC. I've heard all of them hundreds of times. I could do all the voices and still have to be told firmly to stop doing them all the time. When we started out doing kind of multi-voiced things the only example that we had to follow was really *Stan Freberg's History of America* album and our knowledge of *The Goon Show*. There is nothing for sure abstract humour like Spike Milligan's writing. That's it. And of course he had the cast of doom with Harry Secombe, Peter Sellers and himself.

You can't talk about the Goons, I feel, without pointing out that Spike Milligan is the greatest genius of the kind of humour that so neatly enfolds the Firesign Theater. You either like to loon around or you don't. The Pythons looned, for instance, and so does Firesign Theater. We are so in debt to the Goons, all of us, that years ago I just resigned myself to the fact that Milligan is my master and I'm really just following behind him. Perhaps I'm walking backwards for Christmas, across the Irish Sea, but that's Spike up ahead of me and I'll never catch him.

* Others, including Eric Sykes, also seem to have witnessed this incident.

*'*Contraceptives should be used on every conceivable occasion!*'*

 Minnie Bannister

BILL WYMAN

Bill found popularity and fame in the Rolling Stones in the 1960s. His current group, the Rhythm Kings, tours regularly.

As far as I can recall, I first met Spike on 2 March 1984 at Capital Radio where we were both doing different programmes. We chatted and then he agreed to do mine together with me, as I was such a great fan of his work with the Goons and the Q programmes. I'd also known Peter Sellers for some time and we always chatted about Spike when we got together.

My next contact was when he sent me a crazy, amusing telemessage from Australia on 21 October 1985 for my birthday on the 24th.

A year later, he invited me and my girlfriend to dinner at his house in London. We had a lovely meal and then he proceeded to sit at the piano and play and sing little songs for us, which were very charming. It was a wonderful night.

In early 1987, I heard that Spike was thinking of leaving to live in Australia, as they wouldn't give him a British passport. I immediately went to Asprey, where I bought two leather-bound books. I then started getting in touch with all of my music, sport, TV and film contacts and had them sign the books to persuade Spike not to leave. Within a couple of months both books were full

– with drawings, poems and signatures from a whole host of celebrities, from Alec Guinness to Paul McCartney. Jim Davidson helped me on this project.

On 29 May I was on the *Wogan* show with Spike, where I presented the two books to him. We went to dinner afterwards and he sat, reading dedications from all the friends who had contributed, and got quite emotional. We chatted into the early hours.

I appeared on TV with him a few times in the following years and he came to my wedding reception on 5 June 1989, where he presented me with a walking-frame, 'To get you through the honeymoon', as he put it!

In 1996, he attended a charity event at Sticky Fingers, my restaurant, in aid of the Rees Daniels Trust, which was a 'Jokeathon' night. It was attended by others such as Lionel Bart, Twiggy and Bob Hoskins but, needless to say, Spike won the 'Oscar' for the best joke of the night. Then, later that year, he asked me to contribute to his charity for the Elfin Oak at Kensington Gardens, which I was happy to do. So, on 12 June 1997, my wife, Suzanne, and I attended the unveiling together with Sir Paul Getty and Prince Charles. We then had cocktails and lots of laughs before the four of us met up for an hilarious dinner somewhere in Kensington.

We talk on the phone sometimes and Spike is always funny. The last time, about two weeks ago, he commented, 'Are you still alive? I thought you had died!' He also asked me if I still had the walking-frame, which I do.

I think that Spike has been the most original comedian England has ever produced – I love him dearly.

MAUREEN LIPMAN

***The award-winning actress
and writer remembers the
night the Prince was Spiked!***   I was in the audience at the Comedy
Awards Ceremony in 1994, the night
Spike received a Lifetime Achievement Award, and there was a
generous and fulsome tribute from Prince Charles. I don't
suppose Spike had the slightest idea he was going to call his
future King a 'grovelling little bastard', until the words were out
of his mouth. The impulse, though, was irresistible and he gave
in to it without the slightest struggle. There was a moment of
incredibly pregnant silence, followed by roll upon roll of wild
laughter.

As I mopped myself dry I remember thinking that Spike would
have been perfect casting for Lear's Fool. Perfect. He did the
jester's job flawlessly. By living dangerously, without fear for
himself or his position, he pricked the bubble and in so doing he
restored life's proportion for all of us.

His written work, his wit and personal memories will ensure he
is remembered as not just a Goon, but an iconoclastic herald.

P.S. Shortly after the incident, Spike apparently wrote to the
Prince: 'I suppose a knighthood's out of the question now?'

Spike displays the letter from The Prince of Wales congratulating him on receiving a
Lifetime Achievement Award for Comedy, during the 1994 British Comedy Awards.

DIMITRIS VERIONIS

Dimitris is a Greek 'Jack of all trades', including lyricist and writer.

Peter Sellers was the body, Harry Secombe the soul and Spike Milligan the mind of the Goons – this is how I see them. I am Greek and my mother tongue is Greek, yet Spike's humour and sensitivity are so profound that they travel well to other cultures and languages. His art has the rare spirit to awaken the child in us all. His work reminds us what or how we should be, his vision of humanity has no borderlines.

One of Spike's most important abilities is revealing the human race's inner qualities; he looks through a keyhole at us in our nakedness and sees our love, greed, vanity, ambition, foolishness, absurdity, tenderness . . . he sees through us. Moreover, he can describe us better than *we* can!

For me, the Goons were only the beginning in getting to know Milligan's work. Soon I discovered the Q series, Spike the poet, the activist, the novelist and the children's best friend. He seems to have given new dimensions to every field of writing or performing that he has entered. His work has the gift of remaining contemporary and it will always be rediscovered by future generations.

I had the chance to meet Spike Milligan at the unveiling of a plaque with Peter Sellers, at Elstree Studios in July 2000. Maxine Ventham was kind enough to introduce me to Spike and Shelagh. They were both warm and friendly. He asked me where I came from and I told him Athens, Greece. Jokingly, he questioned, 'Why does every Greek I meet tell me that he lives in Athens?' We chatted for a while and then I showed him a Greek magazine I had with me, which featured an interview I had given on Peter Sellers. I tremblingly asked Spike to sign it and he was good enough to do so, ignoring the six pages of the magazine packed with pictures of Peter Sellers and the Goons and signing instead the cover, dragging an arrow down from his name to an image of *Homo sapiens*. Has anyone ever got a better autograph?

Just lately I have discovered Spike, the straight singer, and his wonderful, emotional voice on 'Will I Find My Love Tonight?' I have discovered my wedding song! God bless you Spike Milligan!

DAVID RENWICK

Comedy writer David Renwick has written for The Two Ronnies, *as well as having his own extremely popular series,* One Foot in the Grave *and* Jonathon Creek.

I can just imagine the kind of warm and touching stories you will be able to include, because I know that behind that quirky exterior there beats a highly sensitive heart. Andrew Marshall and I worked with Spike on just one (his final) television series, and for a few years after that would often share a curry with him and Shelagh at their local Indian restaurant in Bushey. I have nothing but fond memories of our time together, and will always regard Spike as one of the few true comedy geniuses of the last century.

Neddie
Seagon

Celebrating with his wife, Shelagh.

S.M. Collection

RICHARD INGRAMS

The editor of the Oldie and former editor of Private Eye recalls his favourite Spike moments.

My favourite Spike story concerns a visit to Dublin in about 1986 to appear on the Gay Byrne chat show on Telefis Eireann. Staying at the Shelbourne Hotel, Spike had ordered dinner to be served in his room after the show. But when it arrived it turned out to be dinner for two rather than one. Typically, Spike invited the waiter to join him and eat the extra dinner. The waiter agreed with alacrity, polishing off the dinner and the bottle of wine that went with it. As he took his leave he told Spike: 'If you don't mind me saying so, sir, I would have thought someone with all your money could have afforded a better bloody dinner than this.' Such things happened all the time to Spike, helping to confirm his view that the world was a crazy place and human beings generally ridiculous. He lived in a state of almost permanent indignation about what went on in the world, but because you cannot live in that state without ending up in a madhouse, he did his best to turn his indignation into jokes.

I was involved with Spike from the time my company Tomorrow's Audience put on *The Bed-Sitting Room* in Canterbury in 1962, the year after *Private Eye* began. Spike supported the *Eye* from the beginning, bombarding the magazine with jokes, cartoons and letters to the editor. After our first big libel action (brought by Randolph Churchill) he wrote complaining that he himself had never been libelled. We obliged by printing underneath his letter: 'Spike Milligan is a dirty Irish poove'. He issued a writ on the ground that he had been called Irish and was awarded damages of 17/6d.

Some years later he inserted a small ad in the *Eye's* classified section: 'Spike Milligan would like to meet rich, well-insured widow. Intention: murder.' He received forty-eight replies.

Anything that happened, anything that was said was turned instantly into a joke. In later years he became a regular attender of the *Oldie* literary lunches at Simpson's. I was sitting next to him at one of those lunches when he suddenly asked, 'Why are they serving bread-and-butter pudding?' 'Because it's Lent, Spike,' I replied. 'When do we have to give it back?' he said, without a second's hesitation. Sometimes he would sit in silence looking rather glum and it was during one of these silences that Barry Cryer tried to cheer him up, whispering, 'You realise, Spike, there are a lot of paedophiles here at this lunch.' Spike looked at him sorrowfully. 'Why do you hate us?' he asked.

At an Oldie *magazine lunch, with it's editor, Richard Ingrams, (centre) and Richard Wilson.*

I was privileged to appear in the original Q5 along with my *Private Eye* colleague John Wells and remember the funniest part being Spike's arguments in front of the audience with the poor producer. Watching a couple of shows from the series recently, I could see why the BBC were so reluctant to repeat them – something that became a bit of an obsession with Spike. The first one I watched featured Spike as a door-to-door salesman trying to sell a housewife (Fanny Carby) a blow-up hunchback as a means of getting the offer of a seat on a crowded train. Throughout the show there was a running joke as follows:

Q: Are you Jewish?

A: No, a tree fell on me.

In our politically correct age the BBC would never show such material in a month of Sundays.

I remember being invited by the BBC to take part in *An Audience With Spike Milligan*, in which we all were provided with questions to ask him from the floor. I tore up the one they gave me and when my turn came asked, 'Spike, are you Jewish?' He gave the right answer, but when the programme was shown our little exchange had been edited out.

'This doesn't necessarily mean you'll paint like Toulouse Lautrec.'

This cartoon by Spike appeared in Private Eye.

Cartoon supplied by Richard Ingrams

At an Oldie *lunch with Peter O'Toole (above), Ian Hislop (centre) and Kenneth Griffith.*

When The Goons ruled the world – a Radio Times cover, November 1957.